A LIKELY STORY

A LIKELY STORY

Reclaiming and applying the Story of the Bible

Brad Peters

Cover photo: Jaredd Craig on Unsplash
Chapters photo: Patrick Tomasso on Unsplash

ISBN: 978-1-7779320-0-8

Dedications

Who knows if I'll get the opportunity to write another book, so I'm going to take full advantage and dedicate this to a few people, all of whom have had a direct influence on everything to follow on these pages.

To my family:

My beautiful wife, Michelle
for providing me with a fairy-tale story of my own, and for inspiring me to want to write a better story for you everyday.

My favourite guitar player, Ceilidh
for reminding me that the best stories are often musical in nature.

My compassionate warrior, Noah
for teaching me that the stories with the most unexpected endings can be the most meaningful.

To my former pastors:

Rev. Dr. Devin Seghers
from whom I borrowed/stole
the sermon-starting question, 'May I tell you a story?'
Rev. Randy McCooeye
for showing me, in word and action, just how deep the story goes.
Rev. Chris Stefanidis
for illustrating, in the very best way, that some of the most effective stories are the ones that make us the most uncomfortable … and for being brave enough to tell those stories.

And of course,

To my Risen Lord and Saviour, Jesus Christ

For being the Master Storyteller, the point of every true story, and the focus of the story of life.

Table of Contents

Table of Contents

Introduction
or
Please don't skip this part of the story

Imagine for a moment that you woke up one morning, took a look at the recent economic news and unemployment numbers and decided that you suddenly had a better ending for John Steinbeck's 'The Grapes of Wrath.'

Or perhaps, after solving the great mystery of who keeps putting the milk container back into the fridge with less than a millimetre of milk in it, you decide you should offer the estate of Arthur Conan Doyle your two cents ... or shillings ... worth of improvements to the endings of the Sherlock Holmes tales.

Both of these situations are, of course, both ridiculous and ludicrous, but there is another story, a far greater story, a far more important story, with an endless barrage of voices trying to rewrite the ending.

That story is the story of the church, the story of the living Bride of Christ.

For the last number of years, there has been a steady stream of articles, pontifications and proclamations all predicting the imminent death of the church.

Those who may only have a superficial understanding of the story, and the power, of the church can be forgiven for their early prognosis of death for the church. After all, with all of the evident problems of the church these days, you don't have to be a medical examiner to realize that something is wrong, that something is sick.

But sick is a long, long way from dead ... as thousands of hospital-bound patients will gratefully attest.

However, we on the inside of the church, we need to be patient with the social and religious critics who are a little too eager to see the Bride of Christ buried and forgotten. It reminds me of that famous, hilarious, Monty Python scene in 'The Quest for the Holy

Grail.' "Bring out your dead," calls the undertaker pulling his "body cart" through the streets. A frail senior citizen is about to be unceremoniously dumped onto the pile on the cart. "Wait, I'm not dead yet," comes the weak cry from the weak old man. "He says he's not dead," Eric Idle's character says to the senior-disposing John Cleese.

"He will be soon. Can't you just take him now?" comes the reply.

If we, as those within the church, are honest with ourselves, we'll have to admit that to the outsider (or like the Cleese character, to those who are just tired of the church), we may appear to be on our last legs.

The stories of massive numbers of churches closing, the statistically significant number of those claiming no religious affiliation (the Nones), punctuated by a seemingly endless string of high-profile pastoral and leadership failures certainly all give the critic a strong opening stance for their argument.

But critics often make the mistake of assuming that the frail, broken, sinful members of the church are the authors of the story of the church, and that's just not true! While those members definitely shape the way the story is presented to the world around us, the author of the story of the church is the One who envisioned her, formed her and died for her - Jesus Christ ... and because Christ is the author, the story continues, and the church continues until the Bridegroom returns for His Bride as confirmed for us in the book of Revelation.

So, our future is certain. The story is still being written by an unshakeable, divine hand, but those criticisms are valid. Idle's undertaker may not be at our door, but we can be forgiven for thinking we can hear the faint echoes of his cart on the cobblestone streets outside our churches. However, we need not despair. As 2 Tim. 1:7 tells us, God has not given to us the spirit of fear, but of power, and of love, and soberness of mind.

I love the phrase "soberness of mind." It speaks to clarity of thought, and control of our thinking. I believe that Paul also chose his words very carefully in writing to young Timothy, wanting him to know that this soberness of thought comes first from a position of power, and a place of love. Again, doesn't that sound just like the Lord Jesus?

We don't need to fear the premature ending of the story of the church, but with power and love, the power and love of Jesus Christ, we must begin to address those symptoms that lead so many around us to flag down the undertaker's cart as they hear it approaching. But how do we do that? How do we reacquaint those both within and without the church of her strength and vitality?

We do this by realizing that we are now living in an age and time when we have three, maybe four generations of entirely "unchurched" people. When I was a child, almost everyone had some connection to church - even if it was just for the "big" holidays of Christmas and Easter. The Roman Catholic kids all knew each other, and we were aware that the other kids attended Protestant churches and public schools. Church was still part of the cultural identification for people in our communities ... but that's just not the case today. So while we cultivated a shared understanding of religious ritual (with clear variations, of course), we also shared a common language and experience, the language of our faith stories.

Sadly, that segment of our collective language, the stories of faith, aren't as well known today. The church must reclaim this reliance on story. We are people of the greatest story ever told, yet so many around us are unfamiliar with this story. But, it's worse than that. People who consider themselves to be part of the church are unsure about the story, and reluctant to tell the story of the One who is love, the One who conquered death, and the One who is the Master Storyteller.

We have to reclaim the power of Story. It's not coincidental that our Jesus, the greatest teacher and preacher of all time, relied on story so heavily in connecting with his audience. He knew the life-changing power of Story. He knew that taking deeply held spiritual truths and wrapping them in tales of both the familiar, and the foreign, resonated with people. In fact, his stories and parables were so well crafted, so true, that they still resonate with people today, people far removed from the cultural, social and economic realities of Jesus' first audiences and congregations.

It's not co-incidental that the Gospel of John begins telling the story of Jesus and his stories by identifying Jesus as the Word. As words are the very building blocks of story, Jesus's story is the foundation of all life.

As that is true, the stories of Scripture still resonate when they are told today. We learn so much about our contemporary lives, and how to interpret the events of this time in the timeless stories of the Old and New Testaments - stories of love, anger, responsibility and avoiding responsibility, of leadership and friendship.

Qoheleth, the writer of Ecclesiastes, tells us that there is nothing new under the sun. In Paul's second letter to Timothy, Paul famously writes that "all scripture is inspired by God and is useful for teaching, for reproof, for correction, and for training in righteousness."

Therefore, it's time again to follow the lead of our Lord, to reacquaint ourselves and others with the power of story, so that we might share the truths that so many around us need to hear.

It's time to reclaim our story by ***telling*** our story, never forgetting that truly, it is the greatest story ever told! That's why I've titled this book, A Likely Story. Usually that phrase is a negative term, one that denotes disbelief, as in: "Sure, that's a likely story." Not only is the Christian story as revealed in the pages of the Bible the defining story of human history, it is, without any negative inference, a likely story … and as I will highlight in the pages to come, it is a highly likeable story.

My final introductory comment is an important one. When I use, as I have been doing, the word 'story', it's crucial that we understand that this is not meant to be interpreted as a fictional tale or a myth. I'm grateful that my pre-ministry career was in journalism, which is where I first developed my love of story. Everyday, journalists and readers dive deep into the truth of the story … and I write this with all certainty, that there is no truer, no more important story than the story of the Good News of Jesus Christ, the story of God involved in the lives of his creation, and the story of the Holy Spirit revealing the truth and love of the Trinity to all people.

Now, may I tell you a story?

Chapter 1

The First Family
or
The (Broken) Ties that Bind

Now the man knew his wife Eve, and she conceived and bore Cain, saying, "I have produced a man with the help of the Lord." Next she bore his brother Abel. Now Abel was a keeper of sheep, and Cain a tiller of the ground. In the course of time Cain brought to the Lord an offering of the fruit of the ground, and Abel for his part brought of the firstlings of his flock, their fat portions. And the Lord had regard for Abel and his offering, but for Cain and his offering he had no regard. So Cain was very angry, and his countenance fell. The Lord said to Cain, "Why are you angry, and why has your countenance fallen? If you do well, will you not be accepted? And if you do not do well, sin is lurking at the door; its desire is for you, but you must master it."

Cain said to his brother Abel, "Let us go out to the field." And when they were in the field, Cain rose up against his brother Abel, and killed him. Then the Lord said to Cain, "Where is your brother Abel?" He said, "I do not know; am I my brother's keeper?" And the Lord said, "What have you done? Listen; your brother's blood is crying out to me from the ground!"

- Genesis 4:1-10 NRSV

"Things were so much better when I was a kid."

"People just don't understand the meaning of family anymore."

"Back in my day, family meant something."

I know that you have heard sentiments like those above expressed. You may have even said those things, or believe these things to be true even now ... and you're probably right. Things probably were a lot better when you were a child: Back before work and a career, before taxes, before responsibility. Of course things were better then, how could they not be?

But that's not what we usually mean when we say or hear comments like these. We're talking about the bigger picture. We're commenting on society. We're referencing the "good old days."

You know, those days of the 1950s nuclear family. The family that looked and sounded a lot like the Cleavers from the 'Leave it to Beaver' TV show - dad wore a suit and tie to work everyday, mom stayed at home and prepared a four-course meal for every dinnertime. The children rarely did anything wrong, but on the rare occasion when they did, after a tormented night of guilt, they always admitted their misdeeds. Sure, there were problem kids around, the 'Eddie Haskells' of the neighbourhood, but even his shenanigans were mostly mild and innocuous ... and besides, those kids were always someone else's children, never ours.

The reality, as most of us know all too well, is that those good old days never really existed. The Cleavers were a packaged, idealized version of what the North American family could, and should, strive to be - good, law-abiding, patriotic contributors to the collective North American dream. Growing up in an average, middle-class family, I certainly didn't know any families as idyllic as those I saw on my television.

Yes, we witnessed love and guidance, instruction and inclusion, but there was also struggle and despair, disappointment, and sometimes, catastrophic failure in the real-life families in the neighbourhood.

One of the beautiful things about the story of God, and God's people, as recorded in the Holy Bible is that it demands that we engage with it honestly and thoroughly. From the very first pages of the Bible, we learn quickly that this will not be a white-wash of the human experience. Mere moments into the human experiment, we are shown for who we are - rebellious liars, cheats and murderers. This is what it meant to be family in the "good old days" when the world was new and God still walked with people in the cool of the day.

So when we find ourselves pining for the good old days, we might want to rethink that idea … or at least make sure that we are in good standing with our brothers and sisters beforehand.

The story of Cain and Abel is probably one of the most well-known sibling rivalry stories in the history of story. But before we get into the details of their story, we need to remember that each and every story also has background. There is a back story, the forming details and the environment in which their story plays out. So let's take a look at mom and dad, Eve and Adam.

The First Family Tree

The first family of God's people had everything they could possible want or need for a successful life. They were given a beautiful garden in which to live, they didn't have to work the land to provide for their daily meals, the rich and abundant provision of God was evident and true for them. This also extended to their spiritual wellbeing. Genesis tells us that God walked with them and that they were able to see God and interact with God in a physical way. When all of their world was new, meaning that everything was still to be learned, they enjoyed a one-on-one tutoring session with the One who made all things - talk about a Master class!

But there's always a cost. There's always a price that must be paid, and what was the cost that Adam and Eve were expected to pay for this unimaginably wonderful existence? Obedience. Love. Honesty. What a shame that the cost for basking in the garden of God's great design for the fulfilled life were the very things that we are seemingly incapable of sustaining for any length of time.

We won't quibble over whose fault it was that Adam and Eve were served their eviction notice for breaking the one requirement that God placed on them, as they both ate of the fruit that was forbidden. They both knew it. They both ate. They both failed. And so, they were both banished from the garden. This is the environment in which Cain and Abel were birthed and in which they grew. So then, we really shouldn't be surprised at how their story unfolds.

It is clear from the opening of Genesis 4 that this is not a generic story about family members, but it is very specifically about brothers.[1] It was more important to the writer of Genesis to identify Abel, not as the son of Adam, but as the brother of Cain. We need to take note of the emphasis on the brotherly relationship. The author mentions the fact that the two are brothers no less than four times over the two verses of verse 8 and 9 in Genesis 4. And why is that important? Because as we move into the part of the story focusing on the offerings of the brothers, I believe that a major part of the narrative focuses on their standing as equals.

There is much speculation on why God accepts the offering of the younger brother, Abel, and not the older Cain. Suggestions have been made that the first-born brother's offering was flawed, that as a farmer, a tiller of the ground, Cain's gift was not up to the standard worthy of God. It is further suggested that Abel, being a shepherd or keeper of the sheep, brought a more substantial offering to the Lord.

Unfortunately, we can't know for sure why God accepted the younger brother's offering and not Cain's. Genesis 4 doesn't specifically indicate the reasons for the rejection, but if we read closely through the rest of the episode, we are given some indication of why this happened. There is no judgmental call given against the quality of the offerings, or whether livestock was a more substantial presentation than the first fruits of the field. In this text at least, they are revealed to be equal offerings, so it must be something else, something not easily visible to the rest of us.

As we read on, God warns Cain of the danger of sin, of anger. Genesis tells us that Cain's "countenance fell," that he was downcast after the rejection of his offering. The NRSV translation tells us that God had no regard for Cain and his offering. It wasn't just the fruit of the field that the Lord was rejecting, but Cain himself. But why? We haven't read of anything to this point that would indicate that Cain is any different, any less than his younger brother or any different than his parents ... and perhaps that's the point. He's not that far removed generationally or spiritually from his disobedient parents. Though he outwardly is going through the motions of honouring God, his heart, as his actions will soon prove, is far from God.

It is said of Jesus in the second chapter of John that he knew what was in the hearts of all men. This is also, of course, true of the

Father. The Holy Trinity of God, the Father, Son and Holy Spirit, share this ability to know, to see, beyond the outward appearance into the very hearts and intentions of humanity. God, looking into the life and the heart of Cain, knew that the presentation of the fruits of Cain's labour was coming from a dark place, not a genuine offering of worship to the Loving Creator God.

The events of Genesis 3 and 4, appear to happen at breakneck speed. No sooner do we observe the introduction of Eve into the Creation narrative, then we read of the deception of the Enemy, the eating of the forbidden fruit, the expulsion from the garden, the birth of the children, the presentation of the offerings, and this chapter in the lives of the first family ends with the murder of Abel. These events of course play out over years, but the pace of the narrative speaks a well-known truth to many of us: When sin is left unchecked in our hearts, it runs away with us - our lives spin out of control.

This escalation in runaway behaviour is captured so frighteningly in Gen. 4:8: 'Cain said to his brother Abel, "Let us go out to the field." And when they were in the field, Cain rose up against his brother Abel, and killed him.'

From a request for company to homicide in the single beat of a darkened heart.

Dysfunction: Then and Now

So what do we do with this? How is this story applicable, and shareable for the church today? Sadly, there are more connection points to this tragic story than we might first like to admit.

One of the major criticisms from those on the outside of the church (as well as those on the inside) is that Christ-followers are hypocritical and "holier-than-thou." The story of Cain and Abel, just one generation removed from the God-created couple, Adam and Eve, should disabuse anyone within the church of this notion of superiority due to our faith. Our ancestors went from walking with God, to hiding from God to running from the Lord in mere moments. This is our spiritual DNA.

One of the greatest descriptions of the church is that it is not just a cathedral for the fortunate, but also a hospital for the spiritually broken and ill. When we view the Genesis story as the creation not just of the world, but also as the formation of God's people, traced from Adam through the patriarchs of the Old Testament to each of us through faith in Jesus Christ, we receive a very clear picture of just how much we need the church to be that hospital.

Instead of holier-than-thou, we need to face the fact that we are all broken, all flawed in some respect or another. That's why this book begins by highlighting this particular story. Everything else that follows in the Bible stems from these first stories. Every other naturally born human profiled in Scripture, as Paul tells us in Romans 3:23, have all sinned and fallen short of the glory of God.

A quick survey of daytime TV talks shows reveals that there is an entire industry that has been built up capitalizing on the tragedy and guilt of people's lives. The most horrific details of life are now packaged, superficially 'dissected' and churned out as talking points for 'experts' to illustrate for us how we can live 'our best lives.' What is sold as self-help instruction is little more than sensationalized gossip.

The church can never let the lesson learned from Cain and Abel be reduced to such pablum. Yes, we have to own our role in this part of our family history. Yes, we have to recognize that we continue to be patients in the spiritual hospitals of our churches.

Again, we learn from Paul from his second letter to the church in Corinth: '(The Lord) said to me, "My grace is sufficient for you, for my power is made perfect in weakness." Therefore I will boast all the more gladly about my weaknesses, so that Christ's power may rest on me.' (2 Cor. 12:8-10)

We admit and own our weakness, our foundational, structural challenges, not so that we can become talk show fodder; not so that we can malign the beauty of the bride of Christ, the church. No, the reasons that we own our fallen nature are twofold: First: To invite all people, regardless of their pasts, into our churches and into our spiritual journeys from a place of broken equality, and 2) we can not navigate this life effectively under our own power. We're not designed to do so. When we share the spotty nature of the origins of God's people, we invite the grace, love and truth of Jesus Christ into our lives. By admitting our weakness - and can there be a greater weakness than being so insecure, so angry, so dark, that one would take the life of a brother? - by admitting this, we allow the power of Christ to focus and redefine our lives.

The story of Abel and Cain reveals not only our weakness, and the potential for violence that not only resides within all of us, but that it can flare into action, deadly action, so very quickly, but it also uncovers our deep need of an active, living God in our lives.

In these days of much-needed accountability, there is one other beautiful revelation about the nature of Yahweh in the opening chapters in Genesis. Just four chapters into the story of God and God's people and we read of lies, deceit, disobedience, and murder. Again, knowing the dark truth of Cain's heart, God's concern is immediately for the victim, for Abel, as expressed in Gen. 4:10: "What have you done?" asks God. "Listen; your brother's blood is crying out to me from the ground!" As we own our role in tragedies, both historic and more recent, we must follow the example of our great God, and listen to the victims of violence and oppression, recognizing and responding to the injustices inflicted upon them.

But there's another reason that we begin this journey through the stories of Scripture with this look at a deeply dysfunctional family. While our family tree has some twisted roots and some knotty (and naughty) branches, it is not without hope. Despite our darkened hearts, and our willingness and ability to lie to the One who gives us life, He loves us still.

Hc pursues us still.

He loves us enough that he has written the most amazing ending to the human story. And we'll discuss that, but there are a few more stories that we need to consider first, including another stop in the Old Testament looking at another important lesson that we learn from another pair of brothers.

Prayer for Our Story

Gracious God, the giver of all good gifts,
We pray for the strength to face our past failures,
And for the strength to move beyond them.

Lord Jesus, the One who uniquely understands the reality of death,
We pray for the strength to accept your perfect sacrifice for us,
And for strength to share that truth with others.

Holy Spirit, the One who reveals the beauty of God to us,

We pray for the ability to find the beautiful image of God reflected in all people,

And for strength to overcome our biases and sinful impulses.

Chapter 2

It's Not Always All about You
or
Why Being Second Banana isn't so Bad

On the day when the Lord spoke to Moses in the land of Egypt, he said to him, "I am the Lord; tell Pharaoh king of Egypt all that I am speaking to you." But Moses said in the Lord's presence, "Since I am a poor speaker, why would Pharaoh listen to me?"

The Lord said to Moses, "See, I have made you like God to Pharaoh, and your brother Aaron shall be your prophet. You shall speak all that I command you, and your brother Aaron shall tell Pharaoh to let the Israelites go out of his land. But I will harden Pharaoh's heart, and I will multiply my signs and wonders in the land of Egypt. When Pharaoh does not listen to you, I will lay my hand upon Egypt and bring my people the Israelites, company by company, out of the land of Egypt by great acts of judgment. The Egyptians shall know that I am the Lord, when I stretch out my hand against Egypt and bring the Israelites out from among them." Moses and Aaron did so; they did just as the Lord commanded them. Moses was eighty years old and Aaron eighty-three when they spoke to Pharaoh.

- Exodus 6:28-7:7 NRSV

We live in an age and a culture where everything around us tells us that we are the focus of everyone around us … or we should be. Right now, either in your pocket, or likely no further than arm's length away is your phone. A device, that with every social media site, app, and photo reel, screams to all who listen, beginning with you of course, that YOU are the star of the show. Every post, every day, is all about you - your day, your preferences, your music, your politics, even your food and meals are showcased. That phone in your pocket is a device unlike any other device ever used in history.

Our smartphones, those mini-computers that often are our link to the online world, are just one onramp onto the superhighway of self-promotion. Social media pages, blogs, Twitter, Instagram, websites and podcasts have taken the job of public relations and self-promotion and literally put it into the palms of our hands.

This isn't an anti-technology rant. I use almost all of the platforms that were listed in the previous paragraph, but I try to do so judiciously. The proliferation and the dangerous conflagration of social media can be a slippery slope for the Christ-follower. As Richard Foster writes, our lives aren't designed for such shameless self-promotion, stressing that "the life we have been created to live is the dynamic, pulsating "with-God life." And Jesus (in his life, death, and resurrection) has made available to you and to me this "life that is life indeed" (1 Tim. 6:19)."[2] The 'with-God' life demands that we echo the sentiments of John the Baptist when he said the Christ must increase, and I must decrease (John 3:30).

But what about my page followers? What about my post likes? I've got to keep my re-tweet numbers up.

Actually, we don't.

One of the greatest stories of the Old Testament is the story of Moses. Told primarily through the first five books of the Bible, known as the Torah or the Pentateuch, we learn that through Moses, God did amazing things. In Moses, God orchestrated wonderful, but sometimes frightening things that not only shaped the early days for God's people, but the ongoing story of both the Old and New Testaments, and the world today.

But here's the astonishing part, especially for an egocentric culture and age like ours, even though Moses was the focal point for the great work of God, it was never about him! In the same way, for those who follow Jesus, as wonderful as the faith-filled life is, despite what social media tells us, in opposition to what the self-help talk shows and their patronizing, mindless advertisements try to sell us, contrary to the claims that buying and owning the latest bit of sleek technology assert, if God is truly God in our lives, then it's not really about us, but it's about God. It's about others. It's about that lifestyle that places the other above ourselves.

Knowing that the work Moses was called to do might lead him to that place where he became less focused on others or on the God that made all the events of the Torah possible, God ensured that Moses would always be part of a ministry team. To make that easier, God kept the early ministry of the Israelites in the family, calling Moses' brother Aaron to join Team Exodus.

So then, it is to the story of Aaron that we turn, a story that teaches us that we don't always have to be No. 1, that top billing isn't the highest goal and that sometimes being a supporting member of the team is more fulfilling than we could ever imagine.

Thanks to Charlton Heston, Yul Brynner and Cecil B. DeMille many people of a certain age are familiar with Exodus story through the classic film, The Ten Commandments. Actually, most people are familiar with the Hollywood version of the Exodus events, cast firmly and almost solely on the broad shoulders of the leading man, Heston. The Ten Commandments was the most successful film the year it was released, 1956, earning an astonishing $122.7 million at the box office, the equivalent of $1.2 billion in today's currency. Now let me ask you a question: Who played Aaron in the film?

It's appropriate as we begin considering the importance of being second, not first, that we recognize that most of us have no idea who played Aaron in the classic film. The actor's name was John Carradine, the patriarch of a well-known acting family in Hollywood. By the time The Ten Commandments was released in 1956, Carradine had already amassed almost as many film credits as Heston would tally in his entire career. By the time of this retirement in the mid-1990s, Carradine had filmed more than three times as many movies as the man who discovered that Soylent Green was people.

To be fair to the movie, and to Carradine, the title of the film was The Ten Commandments, not The Pentateuch, and while making reference to the chosen people entering the Promised Land, the film's focus was on the exodus from Egypt and the receiving of the Law on the tablets from the very finger of God. So, it's not surprising then that we don't receive a fleshed-out picture of the importance of Aaron in the life and ministry of Moses.

So before we examine how the story of Aaron echoes through history to impact us today, let's investigate just who Aaron was. Scripture tells us that Aaron was the older brother of Moses, born three years before his more famous younger brother. We don't know much about Aaron's life before his shared ministry with Moses. Again, from the book of Exodus we read that Aaron was married. His wife was Elisheba, daughter of Amminadab, of the tribe of Judah, with whom he had four sons: Nadav, Avihu, Eleazar, and Ithamar.

Despite Aaron being the first High Priest, and being the founder and ancestor of the Israelite priesthood, the very first time that we read of Aaron is, again, in relation to his brother. God reveals that he is about to free the Israelite people from Egyptian captivity and oppression through Moses. However, the erstwhile Egyptian prince is reluctant to obey God and actually refuses to participate in the plan for freedom. Angry, God informs Moses that Aaron is a good speaker, and that Yahweh would provide and enable Aaron to act as Moses' spokesman.

No. 2 is still a place of privilege

Before we hear again of all that the two brothers would accomplish together, there is one short verse in the Exodus story concerning Aaron that we often overlook. As people of the Book, as Jesus' people, we often take the supernatural and the divine almost for granted, because it is so prevalent in the Word of God, and we, through the present reality of the Holy Spirit in our lives almost become familiar with the move of God in our lives. But we need to stop and realize the enormity of the first interaction between Yahweh and Aaron.

Exodus 4:27 tells us that God spoke to Aaron and that Aaron heard God. Read that again. We are so used to reading that God spoke to this person, or that prophet, that we often just take it in without really considering it. Throughout the 66 books of the Bible, there really are only a few handfuls of people that God spoke to directly, and Aaron was one of the them. The magnitude of this fact should never be lost on us.

Moses, as God's chosen agent of change for the Israelites was always going to be the one on whom the most attention would be given. But that's not to say that the supporting cast, primarily Aaron, would have no role in the unfolding drama of God's people. If that were the case, why would we be talking about him all these years later? And we don't just talk about him, as we'll learn shortly, for those of us who are regular church attendees and participants, we actually are more exposed on a regular basis to aspects of Aaron's impact on the lives and ministry of God's people than his prominent younger brother.

Before the exodus of the people occurs, Aaron, not Moses, is the original vision-caster. Yes, Moses was the one to whom God had given the vision of freedom, but it was Aaron who called the elders of the Hebrews together to begin revealing to them what God was about to do for them.

One of the most astounding, and frightening, aspects of the deliverance of God's people from the oppressive rule of Pharaoh and Egypt were the plagues. We remember with awe and fear the increasing severity of each successive ordeal that Pharaoh's hardness of heart required before the ancient ruler released God's people. Now God, of course, was the initiating agent by which the plagues occurred, but for the first three, by stretching out his staff, Aaron brought on the first three plagues - water of the river turning to blood, an infestation of frogs and the plague of gnats. To make the third plague even worse, there are several schools of thought that indicate that this plague of pestilence may have been even more disgusting, that it may have been a plague of lice.[3]

Aaron is also partnered with his brother to bring about the sixth plague, boils, and helped in delivering the eighth plaque, the locusts. We also have to recognize that Aaron's role in these events is completely supernatural, meaning that he did nothing to initiate or facilitate the reality of the plaques, except for displaying his obedience to be part of the team. These plagues were initiated by God, then mediated by Moses. But Aaron was the device through which they impacted Egypt.

Also noteworthy is the fact that neither of the brothers were spring chickens when this great move of God begins. Moses was 80 years old, and Aaron, being three years older is therefore 83. May the Lord find us all so willing to be obedient and used for such challenging work at any point in our lives, let alone in our twilight years … yet Aaron obeyed.

In addition to the eloquent speeches Aaron gave not only to the Hebrew elders, but to Pharaoh and the Egyptian court, Aaron displayed the great power of God on several other occasions. That staff that he held out to initiate the aforementioned plagues, in other occasions, when Aaron wielded that staff, it changed into a serpent and another time, it was transformed into a blossom and almonds.

Despite all of this, Aaron was never the "main guy." His relegation to second banana status was further cemented following the Israelites' departure from Egypt. He was inconsequential in the march out of oppression, was silent during the crossing of the Red Sea, he sang no victory songs or hymns, and did not feature in the water crisis at Manah.[4] By this time, Moses was definitely the sole leader of the Hebrew people … but that doesn't mean that we are finished hearing about Aaron, or his impact on the faithful today.

Knowing our Place: Then and Now

Forty years is a long time to journey through the desert. A lot of life happens in that amount of time, so of course, Aaron, as brother to Moses, and as high priest, was involved in more than a few more moments of consequence in the unfolding story of God's people. When the Israelites battled the Amalekites, they were winning as long as Moses lifted his hands before the Lord. After a while his hands and arms grew heavy and he needed to lower them, meaning that the tide of battle turned and the Amalekites began winning. To prevent this, and to aid his brother, Aaron and Hur each held one of Moses' arms aloft to ensure the Hebrews would win the battle. (Ex. 17:8-15)

One of the central miracles of the Exodus comes in the form of Jehovah's sustaining provision of food to the Hebrews in the form of the manna that would appear every morning to be collected for the day. It ended up being the dietary staple for the people during their trek through the desert. And again, Aaron finds himself at the centre of this miracle. Exodus 15-16 records the introduction of the manna. Aaron is directed, by Moses, to tell the people of the coming provision from God. In the familiar pattern, God reveals the plan to Moses, Moses tells Aaron and Aaron shares it with the people, but there is an extra duty for the older brother this time. To ensure that the people of God never forgot the divine diet, Aaron is charged with the honour of collecting an omer of manna to be preserved in the ark, "before the Lord," with the tablets of the Ten Commandments.

Yes, Aaron also made some mistakes - some big mistakes, and yes, Moses had to intercede on Aaron's behalf. When Moses was gone longer than expected on Mount Sinai receiving the Tablets,

Aaron caved to the pressure of the people and melted down the gold of the people to form the golden calf idol, a symbol of the growing apostasy among the delivered people. The high priest was neither directly punished, removed nor excluded from the priesthood.

We learn so much from Aaron. We learn, especially from the golden calf episode, that forgiveness is part of life with God. We learn that our worst mistakes, especially those which cause others to value less the Name and Truth of our great God, even those sins can be forgiven.

But, the main lesson that we learn from Aaron is that life with God is not all about us. We are not the star of this story. Aaron shows us that being second does not mean being inconsequential, but it does require us to pursue a deeper level of humility in our lives ... and that is certainly not an easy task in our current egocentric culture.

We see this God-first/others-first model proclaimed and lived out so thoroughly in the life and ministry of Jesus Christ, but it clearly is not just a New Testament concept, as the life of Aaron illustrates. From the earliest chapters of Exodus, Aaron learns of his fate, and his role as servant, not as leader. Exodus 4:17 tells us that God says to Moses: "He (Aaron) indeed shall speak for you to the people; he shall serve as a mouth for you, and you shall serve as God for him."

Aaron serves as a great model for those who would follow Christ, because as this older brother shows us, the life of faith really isn't about us. We affirm this truth with the proclamation that Jesus is Lord, that we willingly, and joyfully, take second place in our lives. Jesus Christ takes the place of prominence. Saying that out loud in this culture reveals how truly counter-cultural an idea this is, and Aaron was a trail blazer in this regard.

Aaron was told early in his ministry that his younger brother would be as God to him. I can only imagine how difficult that must have been for the first-born Jewish son to hear. But he accepted his role, because he knew that God had a greater plan in mind. We see this greater plan continue to be revealed and shared with us as New Covenant believers in the words and teaching of Jesus Christ. In Matt. 20, in the parable of the workers in the vineyard, Jesus ends the teaching with these words that could have built from the life of Aaron: "So the last will be first, and the first will be last." (Matt. 20:16)

There is also one other fundamental thing that we learn from embracing Aaron's willingness to be second, and to embrace being last: The life of the second banana, the life of sacrifice for another, is not without reward. During his flawed life, Aaron was extended grace, he was fortunate enough to have heard Jehovah call his name and lead him into a life of service, which he completed as the first high priest, and he was extended incredible forgiveness for a steep failure of fidelity and leadership.

But with all of his victories and failures, perhaps the greatest benefit from a lifetime of being content with not being the main character in his story was a blessing. And the blessing that Aaron received is one of the most well known prayers and blessings in the entirety of Scripture, thereby making it one of the most oft-repeated segments of worship gatherings around the globe, regardless of Christian denomination. The Blessing of Aaron is the gold standard for benedictions. From Numbers 6:24-26: "The Lord bless you and keep you; the Lord make his face to shine upon you and be gracious to you; the Lord lift up his countenance upon you and give you peace."

If being second banana means being able to give, and receive, blessings like this, that's not a bad place to be, and not a bad position in which to find ourselves.

Prayer for Our Story

Gracious God, we thank you for blessing us and your keeping us.

We praise you that your glorious face does shine upon us, even as we are found building idols in our day-to-day lives.

We are changed by the truth that your beautiful countenance shapes our lives, giving us a peace beyond all understanding.

Lord Jesus, again, the power of your story-telling leaves us in awe.

May you give us the strength to understand the necessity of being last so that others may be first.

May our joy be in the present reality of seeing your life and love in the lives of those we endeavour to serve and lift before you.

Holy Spirit, the one who reveals the heart of God to us,

Enable us to embrace a life of service to the other.

Change our hearts so that we may unabashedly live a life that is not about us.

Chapter 3

Intentional Self-deception
or
The Prophet of Profit and the Journey on a Jenny

Then the angel of the Lord went ahead, and stood in a narrow place, where there was no way to turn either to the right or to the left. When the donkey saw the angel of the Lord, it lay down under Balaam; and Balaam's anger was kindled, and he struck the donkey with his staff. Then the Lord opened the mouth of the donkey, and it said to Balaam, "What have I done to you, that you have struck me these three times?" Balaam said to the donkey, "Because you have made a fool of me! I wish I had a sword in my hand! I would kill you right now!" But the donkey said to Balaam, "Am I not your donkey, which you have ridden all your life to this day? Have I been in the habit of treating you this way?" And he said, "No."

- Numbers 22:26-30, NRSV

Numbers chapter 22 contains one of the funniest, oddest stories in the entire Bible. However, beyond the chuckles that a seemingly obstinate she-donkey provides, this story reveals some deep truths that speak in profound ways to many of the issues that we deal with today. Among the lessons of relevance are comments on our love of money, the willingness to sell God out for a payday, nationalism, the questionable treatment of animals, and genuine faith in Jehovah.

You probably noticed that in the above paragraph, I included two lessons involving money. This probably isn't a surprise for many of you who are familiar with your Bibles, and the teachings of our Lord Jesus. It's not surprising because money, and its place of importance in our lives and in our hearts, was a recurring theme in Jesus' teaching ... and Balaam, in this story from Numbers sheds light on just how correct and accurate Jesus' lessons were and are.

There is a well-known story about the impacts of money on the faithful, and how money blinds us to the needs of God's people.

A rabbi tells the story of one faith community, in which there was a very rich, but 'frugal' member of the congregation, who refused to donate to the temple building fund. The rabbi invited the man into his study, directed him to the window and asked him what he saw through the window.

"People," came the reply.

The rabbi then asked the man to look into a mirror and to share what he saw.

"Myself," was the answer.

The rabbi responded: "Isn't it funny that the window is glass, and the mirror is glass. The only difference is that the mirror is covered with a little silver. Whenever you add a little silver to the situation, you no longer see others, only yourself."[5]

The desire for money, power and prestige has long been one of the primary obstacles to a fulfilled life with God. Numbers 22 tells us that this is not just a modern-age, 21st-century struggle. Neither is money the only situation that this chapter and the second-most famous donkey in the Bible forces us to consider. To get the full weight of why and how this chatty Jenny becomes so important to the story, and to us, we need to consider the context of these verses.

As this story occurs in the middle of the Book of Numbers, the first thing that we need to recognize is that the shadow of Moses looms large over these events. Although the name of Moses is not mentioned in this passage, the personality and character of Moses is the backdrop against which we see Balaam's nature revealed, and by the end of this episode we find the comparison most unflattering to the pagan prophet.

A Story of Numbers in Numbers

The first 10 chapters of the fourth book of the Pentateuch are action-packed, which I know is not normally a description of this book. Here's a quick synopsis of the story: God's chosen people, having been delivered from Egypt are camped at Mount Sinai as Moses has ascended the mountain to receive the Law from the very fingertip of God. With the messy business of the golden calf and the punishment of the people behind them, and with the ark of the covenant before them, they took a census of the people, set the orders of encampment and marching, and embarking with military precision, they continued the journey to the Promised Land.

Twelve men, one from each tribe, were selected as scouts or spies to travel ahead of the people. As they scouted the area ahead, all of the 12 spies reported a great and prosperous land awaited ahead, land in which the people would prosper. However, 10 of the 12 covert operatives were fearful of the Canaanites. They suggested the people would not be able to defeat the Canaanites, and the fearful Israelites refused to move into that land, even though Jehovah, who pledged His protection for them and presence with them, had promised the land to them.

What was the result for this rebellion, this deviation from the plan of God? Divine punishment. The sentence for their crime of unbelief was 40 years of wandering in the desert until that entire generation had died off. By the time we reach Chapter 20 of Numbers, the second generation of those freed from Egypt have taken hold. As the Israelites approach the land of Moab, imagine the size and scope of this mass of people bearing down on the border. It's no wonder that the Bible describes the Moab people as being fearful, filled with dread at the coming of Israel.

Quaking with fear, Balak, the Moabite king, took a quick survey of his options. Should he send in the Moabite army? It was not nearly big enough. Negotiation (also known as politely asking them to go away)? Not likely. So, he resorts to the fail-safe plan for the ancient near-Eastern mind - divination. He'll get someone to curse the approaching Israelites to make them vacate Moab territory. Enter Balaam … and eventually, his donkey.

The Profit Prophet

Balaam was renowned as a seer, as a man of supernatural influence. He was from Pethor, in a community that was the centre "of a complex cult of prophets and seers whose activities precisely resemble those of Balaam. The fact that he undoubtedly represented the prophetic customs and practices of (the) vicinity makes possible a better understanding of Balaam's narrative in Numbers."[6] Balaam was the answer to the question, 'If you need someone cursed, who you gonna call?'

In an irony that we will discuss a little further into this section, one of the primary strengths of the pagan seer's bag of tricks was his ability to use animals as part of his divinations. His animal sorcery included the dissection of animal livers, interpreting the movement of animals and the flights of birds.[7] How wonderful ironic that this great pagan sorcerer was unable to predict, discern, or even prevent the upcoming movements of the very animal he would be riding upon.

Balak sends envoys to convince Balaam that he must curse the approaching Israelites to prevent them from descending upon Moab and taking over. The envoys carry with them the payment required for Balaam to intercede on their behalf, and they ask him to do just that. Before answering, Balaam invites them to get comfortable, stay the night and he would let them know in the morning ... after he talks it over with God.

It's important that we understand how odd that aspect of the story is. Balaam is not a Jewish prophet. He is not part of the chosen people of God. He is in the business (and business was good), of using any and all deities for his own benefit. With no allegiance, or even relationship that we are aware of, he approaches Yahweh and says, 'The Moabite king is going to pay me for cursing the people that you have blessed, are you all right with that?' (Numbers 22: 7-12)

Not surprisingly, God answers with a resounding, 'NO! I'm not all right with that." But that's not exactly what Balaam tells the Moabites. He tells them that the Lord has refused to allow him to travel with them, but interestingly, he neglects to share that Yahweh has prohibited him from cursing his beloved people.

Even with a lucrative payday on the line, Balaam returns to the Moabites and says, 'Sorry, no can do,' and he sends the envoys back on their 370-mile, 20 to 25-day journey returning to Moab. Was this just a negotiation tactic for an even bigger cheque? Perhaps. The weary travellers pack up, head home and report to the king, who is NOT pleased to learn the sorcerer is not with them. Instead of formulating a different battle plan, he doubles down on the Balaam front, sending a larger, more prestigious delegation with a "blank cheque/name your price" promise to come curse the ever-approaching Israelites.

Balaam must have been enticed by the offer, because even though he heard God clearly say no the first time, he invites the delegation to again spend the night so that he might inquire of the Lord. This time, God relents, permits Balaam to travel with the Moabites, if they come to get him in the morning, but he must only say to them the words that Yahweh gives to him to speak. The problem is that nowhere in the text do we read that the dignitaries actually came to convince Balaam to leave with them. God said if, but Balaam sees that blank cheque, gets up early and prepares to leave.

Saddle up the donkey, because we're off to Moab, and it's on this journey that we learn so much that resonates for us today.

Jenny from the Block

With visions of glory and gold in his mind, Balaam sets out with his two servants and the star of the story, the donkey. But Yahweh is not pleased that the sorcerer didn't listen carefully to his instructions, and so he sends an angel to block the road as an adversary. Of course, Balaam is completely unaware of the messenger from God standing immediately before him, with a sword of holy righteousness in the angel's hand ... but the donkey knows.

How wonderfully poetic that this renowned "seer" is completely unable to see the Messenger of the Lord standing before him, but the donkey can see. As we move into this part of the story of Balaam, another important message is presented to us: When we don't know God, we miss seeing God all around us, and God ***is*** all around us. Sometimes, a manifestation of God appears in the very road before us ... if we would only have eyes to see and ears to hear.

Imagine seeing this encounter and interaction between Balaam and his donkey from the perspective of Balak's emissaries. How foolish the great prophet must have appeared to them. They must have laughed at this famous seer, renowned for his animal-parts divination, unable to see a way to make the beast of burden behave. When Balaam's eyes are fully opened, and he witnesses the Messenger of the Lord standing before him, he does the only sensible thing, and falls facedown on the ground, prostrate before the angel. But it's doubtful his travelling companions saw the angel, all they see is this 'prophet' who can't control a she-donkey, now facedown in the dirt. They must have been wondering, "Balak sent us all this way for this? This man is insane."

The donkey attempts to take Balaam away from the armed angel three times. The first sees Jenny re-routing the seer off the road and into the open field beside the road. When the regular urging and prompting the animal back onto the road doesn't work, the vicious beating and threats begin. After beating the animal back onto the road, the donkey sees the angel again, just as they were passing walls on the other side of the road. Veering to one side, the donkey pins and scrapes Balaam's leg and foot against the wall. The beating resumes. The third time, the angel leaves no way past, so the donkey simply lies down in the middle of the road. With ego and foot equally bruised before King Balak's messengers, Balaam fairly loses his mind in abusing the animal. It's likely that the only sounds that were louder than the seer's curses were the painful bleatings of the dormant donkey.

And then the impossible happens.

The donkey talks!

Read that again. The donkey spoke! As incredible as that is, Balaam doesn't even blink an eye at this wrinkle in the journey. The donkey understandably wants to know why she is being beaten in that way. The answer? "Because you've made a jackass out of me before these dignitaries!"

Unaware that his faithful donkey was only trying to save his life, this gives us real insight into the character and ability of this seer. Was this not a man who was supposed to be in touch with spiritual realities? Yet he's shown up on that front by a donkey … not an animal known for its intellectual acuity. The angel, unable to bear the abuse of this situation any longer, speaks up, and asks, "Why are you beating this poor animal so ruthlessly?"

In the angel's voice and question, Balaam is beginning to understand that this is not just any other money-making, prophet-for-hire job. He admits to the angel that he has sinned, and that if required by God, he would return to his home, but there is more for Balaam, and us, to learn. In the threatening and cursing of the donkey, Balaam was in effect cursing the only blessing that he had in that moment. If not for Jenny the Talking Donkey, the angel's sword of righteousness would have cut through him like a hot knife through butter.

The connection between Balaam, the donkey and Israel is clear. Israel was the recipient of God's promise of blessing, and that blessing was extended to all of creation - including you and me - through Israel. Balaam was actively and intentionally seeking to twist that blessing into a curse and by doing so was bringing that curse onto himself. Just as he almost had with his amazing talking mule.

This passage teaches us clearly that we best be for what God is for and that there is real and genuine danger of being against that which God is for.

But all is not lost for Balaam ... or for us. It is a fair assumption that he travelled with Balak's entourage as a potential way to line his wallet. Money is certainly an influential factor in this story, but even though he travels to curse, when confronted with the glory of God as reflected in the sheer size of His gathered people, the Israelites, on the Moab border, any potential curses become blessings.

In that moment, when financial considerations are laid aside, and Balaam focuses on something bigger, something truer than gold and silver, the prophet of profit becomes a genuine prophet of God.

And we shouldn't be surprised by this change of heart, or this elevated understanding. Time after time, in message after message, Jesus stresses the need to have a proper, healthy relationship with money and finances. The rich young ruler of Mark 10:17-27 illustrates the struggle and difficulty of balancing the spiritual with the monetary. But for those of you who may be thinking that perhaps Jesus was a little too harsh on this rich, young man with clear good intentions, there is a test that the Lord gives to us. Find yourself a camel. I'm sure the local petting zoo can help you out. Break out your sewing kit, and pick the biggest needle you can find. Now, take your borrowed camel and shove, coax, or cajole the dromedary through the eye of that needle. Take your time, it may be difficult. Jesus says it is easier to move that large, lumbering animal through that needle's eye than for a rich person to enter the kingdom of God. (Matt. 19:24)

Years later, Paul comments on this age-old problem to young Timothy when he counsels his protege that love of money is the root of all kinds of evil (1 Tim 6:10). Sadly, we know that these roots run deep, and we have seen many kinds of evil spring up all around us in our time. Even a cursory look at many of the pastoral and church leadership scandals that have rocked the church, and the faith of many individuals, will reveal that if money wasn't the major motivating factor in said scandal, it often contributed to, or was evident in, the revealed moral failure.

But thankfully, and graciously, because God is the God of the second chance (and the third, and the fourth...), this failure doesn't have to be the end of the story. Like Balaam, if we look with new eyes on the situations that are before us, the majesty of God can change us. The Kingdom of God, being revealed all around us, in both magnificent and mundane ways, is more than powerful enough to lead us into a new direction of faithfulness. It was certainly true for Balaam, who found himself unable to speak anything other than blessings onto God's people, regardless of the personal cost.

The same can be true for us. There is a way through the eye of the needle. In fact, there's only one way through, and it's via the Cross of Christ. Jesus, crucified and resurrected, has the power to change everything, and everyone. Even the rich, you ask? Yes, even them, because when a person comes into a genuine relationship with the Risen Lord, they are no longer defined by the size of their bank accounts, but by the size of their hearts. The truth is that all in Christ are wealthy people ... and some of them even have money. The difference is that while some Christians may have money, money does not have them!

It was mentioned in the first part of this chapter that the story of Balaam and the talking ass featured the second-most famous donkey in the Bible. The first, of course, was the donkey that the Lord Jesus sat astride as he rode into Jerusalem on Palm Sunday, fulfilling the prophecy of Zechariah. As a concluding thought on this chapter, and the lessons learned from Balaam, we should be ever-vigilant about our motives, our true loves, and the desires of our heart. In Jesus, we find one who hears God speak, and responds, 'Yes, Father.' In Balaam, we find one who hears God speak, and responds, 'Yes, Father ... but if I ask again, might I receive a different answer?'

If we find ourselves intentionally manipulating God's clear direction for us, we might be well served by asking ourselves, as Balaam should have: Who is the ass here?

Prayer for Our Story

Gracious God, we thank you for your blessing and for keeping us.

We praise you that through your chosen people you have blessed us, and you bless us still.

We stand in awe of the truth that you will go to any lengths, no matter how inconceivable or unlikely to connect with us.

Lord Jesus, You Lord, are the living proof of the great length our Father will go to reach us.

May we always be focused on your leading, your pre-eminence in the ordering of our lives. When power or money draws our attention away from you, away from the Cross, may we remember how all things pale in comparison to you.

May we heed well and seriously the words that you spoke to us of not letting money master us. May we always choose to serve you over our financial portfolios.

Holy Spirit, the one who reveals the ever-working heart of God to us,

Enable us to discern the spiritual realities that are unfolding around us all the time.

Change our hearts so that we heed both the 'Yes' and the 'No' of our great God.

Chapter 4

Whale Interiors
or
The Dangers of Running from our Problems

Now the word of the Lord came to Jonah son of Amittai, saying, "Go at once to Nineveh, that great city, and cry out against it; for their wickedness has come up before me." But Jonah set out to flee to Tarshish from the presence of the Lord. He went down to Joppa and found a ship going to Tarshish; so he paid his fare and went on board, to go with them to Tarshish, away from the presence of the Lord. But the Lord hurled a great wind upon the sea, and such a mighty storm came upon the sea that the ship threatened to break up. Then the mariners ... picked Jonah up and threw him into the sea; and the sea ceased from its raging ... But the Lord provided a large fish to swallow up Jonah; and Jonah was in the belly of the fish three days and three nights.

- from Jonah 1, NRSV

Running away.

We've all done it, or wanted to do it. Often the running away happens in our childhood. We're usually mad at our parents because they make life unbearable by refusing to let us do exactly what we want, when we want, how we want. Who is mom to tell you that you can't jump off the roof in that Batman costume, anyway?

We've all seen the illustrations of the young child with a satchel tied on the end of a stick containing all the worldly possessions of the young - toys, comics, and usually, a lunch packed by that same stubborn woman who dragged you off the top of the house while the rest of the pint-sized neighbourhood Justice League watched.

Of course, that desire to run away doesn't just evaporate when you outgrow the Caped Crusader or Wonder Woman outfit. That feeling of fleeing, leaving responsibilities behind, for the always greener pastures, that draw, that pull, it surfaces every once in a while. Perhaps we aren't as far from that previously mentioned rooftop as we might like to think.

As adults, when are we likely to run away? Usually when someone makes our life unbearable by, you guessed it, refusing to let us do exactly what we want, when we want, and how we want. And who are they to tell me I can't do what I want anyway, I'm a fully-grown adult, aren't I?

'We Run' is more than just a great '80s song, it's one of the ways that we often deal with conflict. We run when we don't like the options, when confrontation is likely, especially if it's likely to be unpleasant. We run if we are scared or uncertain of the outcome. Mirroring and exploring our desire to flee from our discomfort are scenarios that are played out over and over again in our artistic expressions. This inner conflict clearly makes for great art.

But why does our desire to run make such great fodder for art? Because it's true, it's real and it's universal. It is something to which we can all relate - from our reluctance to face what's ahead of us has come some of our most enduring art. From E.M. Forster's 'A Room with a View' to C.S. Lewis' 'The Lion, The Witch and the Wardrobe' to more modern fare including the above mentioned Strange Advance song to the wonderfully rich and detailed graphic novel, 'The Sandman' from Neil Gaiman, running from our problems, be they financial, emotional, spiritual, or as is often the case, a combination of all three, seems to give credence to the suggestion of a recurring flight response.

So with the prevalence of fleeing in the human story, it's not at all surprising that we also find an example of running away in the Bible. In Jonah, and his story, we not only find an example of running away, but we find THE story of running away.

Long-Distance Runner

From the very opening words and sentences of the Book of Jonah, we are given indicators that we are in for a bumpy ride. Jonah, the book, is a story about a prophet, but not primarily about his prophecies, even though the four-chapter Old Testament entry begins in similar fashion to many other prophetic books. It begins, 'Now the word of the Lord came to Jonah, son of Amittai.' We have the divine directive, the in-reaching of God's word, the name of the prophet, and his family connection. But then things get a little weird.

"Go to Nineveh and cry out against it," says God. At this point in our Bible reading, we expect the prophet, the one chosen by God to speak the words of Yahweh. God says go, and the typical response has the prophet responding in obedience to that direction. The book of Jonah begins that way, and we are expecting Jonah to follow the obedience pattern: "And Jonah rose up …" but instead of completing the act of obedience to proclaim the word of God to the Ninevites[8], the author writes, "But Jonah set out to flee to Tarshish from the presence of the Lord." (Jonah 1:3)

"No," says Jonah, and packs a suitcase and starts heading in the opposite direction.

John Goldingay calls Jonah "the stumbling prophet."[9] What an apt description for the man who would foolishly try to run away from God. Just where did Jonah think he could run to that would be hidden from God? And where do we think we can go when we do the same thing? The truth from Psalm 139:8-10 that applied to Jonah's situation applies to ours as well:

Where can I go from your spirit?
Or where can I flee from your presence?
If I ascend to heaven, you are there;
if I make my bed in Sheol, you are there.
If I take the wings of the morning
and settle at the farthest limits of the sea,
even there your hand shall lead me,
and your right hand shall hold me fast.

Tarshish wasn't far enough for Jonah to evade God. Our journeys into the worlds of self-deception, self-delusion, substance abuse or other forms of self-harm never take us beyond the scope or attention of God. Yet still we run … and still Jonah ran.

As much as the story of Jonah illustrates the futility of running away from our problems - especially if that problem is spiritual in nature with God at the centre of the situation - the short book of

Jonah also highlights so very clearly for us what amazing things can happen if we stop running from God's direction. We are given a bird's eye (and whale's stomach) view of just what lengths the Creator God is willing to go for us, and to see his plan fulfilled.

The New Testament reveals Jesus Christ to be the Lord of all things, including the created world. Several episodes in Scripture reveal Jesus to be Lord over the natural order, including the wind and the waves. As Christ is the physical manifestation of God, we shouldn't be surprised to find several episodes in the Old Testament revealing that Yahweh also has strict control over his created world, and here again in Jonah, we read that God also controls the wind and the waves. Like Father, like Son.

It fits the occasionally humorous vibe of this story that for Jonah, the calm before the storm of the great prophet-swallowing fish was literally a storm. When the calm before the storm is literally a potentially deadly storm, perhaps it's time to rethink your life choices. God shows that he is willing to chase Jonah down for the benefit, not just of the prophet, but of the city of Nineveh. So, the Lord of wind and waves unleashes a zephyr on steroids.

The storm was so intense that seasoned sailors were afraid, calling out to their deities - to no avail. They were chucking cargo over the side in an attempt to lighten the load so they might outrun the storm - no luck here either. While all this is going on, our reluctant prophet continues his game of hide and seek with God by trying to hide in the realm of the unconscious - he's sleeping as a life and death scenario is unfolding on the deck above him.

Roused from his sleep by the captain with an urgent call to prayer, the crew soon learns that it is Jonah, and his God, that is the reason for the maelstrom. After a quick round of casting lots, the crew fearfully toss the man of God into the raging sea. Immediately, the sea calms, and the crew make new commitments to God (after all, there are no atheists in foxholes ... or sinking cargo ships, apparently), and they carry on their way to Tarshish, leaving Jonah bobbing in the sea like so much fish food.

So the crew is safe, and Jonah is still able to avoid the direction of God, right? Wrong. I didn't suggest that Jonah was fish food for no good reason. Enter the whale ... or rather, Jonah enters the whale.

The "inside" seat

To say that this is a fantastic part of the story is an exercise in understatement. In fact, it's so amazing that people throughout history have often questioned whether this story is meant to be taken as historical or as an instructional parable. There are good arguments on either side of the debate. I'll let you make up your own mind on how to process this story, just make sure that you do process this story because it still says so much to us today.

So the sailors pitch the prophet overboard to save their skins. And it works. The last thing Jonah may have seen before being swallowed by the great fish was the tail end of the ship Tarshish bound. It's important that as we move to the interior of the Jonah story that we keep in mind that spending a few days being slowly digested by the great fish was not meant as a punishment for our wayward prophet. Verse 17 of chapter 1 tells us that the Lord "provided" the large fish to swallow up Jonah.

As we turn into Chapter 2 of Jonah's story, it appears at first blush that we finally hear the prophet acting like a prophet. He's actually praying, and even better, it's a prayer of thanksgiving. He recognizes that it was the gracious, loving nature of God that resulted in his rescue, but we also have to remember that Jonah is a rebel and a runner. Grab your Bibles and read through the prayer of Chapter 2. While there is definitely gratitude being expressed there, do you know what we won't find there?

Responsibility.

There is no acceptance of his role in this predicament. Jonah seems unwilling or unable to identify his part in the predicament in which he finds himself. While we are considering just how truthful this prayer may or may not be as a genuine reflection of the prophet's heart, this may be a good time to talk about his name.

Our whale passenger's full name means "dove, the son of truth." The son of truth. We might think that a prophet, especially one named the son of truth, would know the very Voice of Truth when he heard it. Further, it's a fair assumption to make that the son of truth would not only know the Voice of Truth when he hear heard it, but he would obey that Voice. The trip to Tarshish is the first clue that this is just not the case with Jonah. When we consider this Chapter 2 prayer, it's clear that Jonah is also not able to be true to himself.

Think back to those times when you've wanted to leave, to run. Part of the reason that we often feel that need to get away is because we aren't being honest with ourselves. It's easier to run than to face the situation that is plaguing us. But as Jonah learned, and like most of us eventually learn, we can't run away from ourselves. It's like trying to run away from the clothes you are wearing. We may leave the site of the situation, but we take the troubles with us. We can either face them, get on with recovery and improve our situations, or we keep living in denial. Jonah, even through this prayer of thanksgiving, was still living in denial.

I find it funny that it's after this sorry/not sorry prayer of the prophet, that the Lord has the great fish vomit Jonah on the dry land. It's almost as if hearing the man evade the one thing that needs to be said in that prayer was enough to make the fish sick, and up comes Jonah.

Upon receiving the second call from God to go to Nineveh and warn them of the judgement to come, we get to the heart of this story. We finally learn why Jonah was running from his work and from God. He didn't want to share the message because he feared that the people of Nineveh might actually listen to him and change their ways. If that happened, God, being gracious and loving, would forgive and give Nineveh another chance. Jonah didn't want to be heard by the Ninevites. Jonah didn't want God to be gracious. Jonah didn't want anything other than what Jonah wanted. But as we learned earlier in Chapter 2 with Aaron, it's not about Jonah. Just like it's not about us.

When we run from our problems, we are running from ourselves. We are running from God in two ways. First, we are running from who God has made us to be, and then we are avoiding the very nature of God. When you think back over all of the reasons that have been mentioned for that running instinct, how many of them are reflective of the nature of God?

None of them.

How many of them are contrary to the person and character of God? All of them. Every single one of them. We run from anger, hate, envy, jealousy, fear, and sometimes, as Jonah illustrates, out of maliciousness. We find none of those characteristics in our great and holy God, and because all people are designed for connection and community with the creator God, when we can't sync our desires with the nature of God, we either submit … or, you guessed it, we run.

The last chapter of this short book turns from the slightly humorous to the overtly sad. How disappointing that anyone could wish the utter destruction of another rather than joyfully and passionately work for their good. Against all odds, the entire city of Nineveh, from richest to poorest, from the most noble to the most common, even the animals exhibited a change of behaviour wanting to please the God of this angry, sullen, smells-like-fish-innards messenger. Does the prophet rejoice? Amazingly, no!

What does he do? He heads east out of the city, tries to find a good vantage point to see if God will wipe out the city. Seeing his messenger fretting in the sun waiting for the destruction that wasn't coming, God provides a bush for shade … for a day. The Lord giveth, and then the Lord taketh away. This is the last straw for our petulant prophet.

After 40 days of shouting himself hoarse about the coming judgement, Jonah wanted some payback on these enemies of Israel. The whole time that he's walking the Assyrian streets, God's self-description of Himself from Exodus 34:6-7 must have been running through Jonah's mind: The Lord is a gracious God and merciful, slow to anger and abounding in steadfast love, forgiving iniquity and transgression and sin. But Jonah is hoping against hope that he's wrong, that somehow God's gracious nature won't surface.

Once again, Jonah is running from the truth.

Swimming Against the Current: Then and Now

The Book of Jonah is so much more than just the historical record of God's warning and mercy to a community that had earned the ire of the Almighty. This story is for us. It is a mirror that helps us to examine our spiritual allegiances, a spotlight that helps us isolate the darkness that exists within all of us … and this story forces us to grow up a little, to silence that nagging little voice that still tells us that running away is not only the easiest option, but the best option.

There's a noteworthy observation on the Book of Jonah that makes it applicable for all of us. J. Denny Weaver, in his wonderful book, The Nonviolent God, argues that the story of Jonah is a parable.[10] Weaver suggests that Jonah represents the unfaithful people of Israel, who are punished by captivity in Babylon, the great fish. They are returned to Palestine, shown in being spewed back onto the shore for another opportunity to be the people God created them to be.

They continue to disobey, reflected by Jonah's continuing and puzzling anger and through this all, God continues to interact and work with Israel as a merciful God.

The application of this story as a parable can certainly speak to areas of our lives, but I would caution against viewing this story strictly as parable. I think the simple but overarching trajectory of the Jonah tale needs to be mirrored in our lives: Specifically, the move from disobedience to obedience. While it's true that Jonah did not make that journey joyfully or graciously, it is nonetheless a story in which we find a glimmer of hope. Hope that we too can move from being inclined to run from God to growing into those willing to stay and interact with the Creator God. It's that aspect of hope that we find Jesus further developing for us in regards to our walk with God.

Jesus knew full well the importance that this little four-chapter book holds in the lives of the believers. In Matthew 16, the

Pharisees and Sadducees are pressing Jesus, demanding that he present to them a sign from heaven. He responds that they are wise enough to determine realities about the physical world, but despite their training and education, they remain ignorant as to the presence of spiritual truths and realities literally standing right there in front of them!

No sign will be given, says the Lord, except the sign of Jonah.

The wisdom and beauty of Jesus' mind and teaching is on full display here. Once again, we have an incredibly complex, nuanced answer with many levels to examine and consider. Here in Matthew, we can easily deduce from our vantage point in history, that it is easy to see that Jesus was referring to the three days he would spend in the tomb. This sign of Jonah is clearly the death and resurrection of the Lord. However, in the recording of this exchange in Luke 11:29-32, it is equally clear that Jesus' answer is meant to evoke the image of Jonah as a prophet preaching and demanding repentance.

You want a sign from heaven? It's right here, in the person of Jesus Christ. As he tells us in the conclusion to the Lukan version of this event, someone greater than Solomon is here. Someone greater than Jonah is here. Not far away in space and time, but here in this moment, in this place.

Stop running away, everything you need is found here, in him. In the answer that is Jesus Christ.

Prayer for Our Story

Gracious God, we thank you for your blessing and your keeping us.

We praise you that truly you are the God who is gracious and merciful, slow to anger and abounding in steadfast love, forgiving iniquity and transgression and sin.

We seek forgiveness for the fact that we are often next in a long line of leavers, of runners. Too often, we wrongly feel that you are not enough, that your way is too hard, that leaving is easier. Forgive us, Father God.

Lord Jesus, You Lord, are the living sign of Jonah amongst us still. When you faced the severest of all trials, you did not run. You taught us what it means to stay.

When we reflect on graciousness and steadfast love, Lord, may we always picture you. May the events of your ministry, your life and your death, may these be those formational truths in our lives.

We pray for the wisdom to run to you, not away from you, when you call us to obedience, when you call us to follow. We pray joy for the journey, that we may find it, and that we may share it.

Holy Spirit, the one who reveals the beauty and depth of Scripture to us,

Give us the strength of the psalmist, who was learning the importance of self-awareness in faithfully following God.

With the psalmist, we pray that you would, 'Search me, O God, and know my heart; test me and know my thoughts. See if there is any wicked way in me, and lead me in the way everlasting.'

Enable us to discern our weaknesses. Enable us to submit them to you and to lay them down.

Change our hearts from places of leaving, to committed and faithful houses in which you can reside.

Chapter 5

You've got a friend in me
or
Why the life of faith isn't meant to be lived alone

When David had finished speaking to Saul, the soul of Jonathan was bound to the soul of David, and Jonathan loved him as his own soul. Saul took him that day and would not let him return to his father's house. Then Jonathan made a covenant with David, because he loved him as his own soul. Jonathan stripped himself of the robe that he was wearing, and gave it to David, and his armour, and even his sword and his bow and his belt. David went out and was successful wherever Saul sent him; as a result, Saul set him over the army. And all the people, even the servants of Saul, approved. ... Saul spoke with his son Jonathan and with all his servants about killing David. But Saul's son Jonathan took great delight in David. Jonathan told David, "My father Saul is trying to kill you; therefore be on guard tomorrow morning; stay in a secret place and hide yourself. I will go out and stand beside my father in the field where you are, and I will speak to my father about you; if I learn anything I will tell you."

- 1 Samuel 18:1-5, 19:1-3, NRSV

History and literature have given us some great stories of friendship throughout the years: Mark Twain and Helen Keller; J.R.R. Tolkien and C.S. Lewis; Mozart and Haydn; Frodo Baggins and Samwise Gamgee; Sherlock Holmes and Dr. Watson; Woody and Buzz Lightyear.

We all long to have that special friend to whom we could sing (or have sung to us) those great lyrics from Randy Newman, "You've got a friend in me."

But why is that? What is it about us that creates that need, that longing, for friendship? There are a couple of reasons for this, and we'll unpack a few of them through this chapter. The first reason, of course, is that we are all made in the image of God - the Triune God. As God is Three-in-One and One-in-Three, community of the deepest sort is intrinsic of God's nature. As we reflect that image of God, we have the longing for that same sort of community, the need for that deep connection. While that desire can only be fully satisfied by knowing God, we are still able and intended to connect in meaningful ways with others on this side of heaven.

As this is a book about our stories, and the Scriptural stories, we must then, as the opening line in this chapter suggests, view this in terms of story. Every great story needs companions, and our stories are no different. As people of story, we are hard-wired to seek the foundational connections of friendships. Our friends are influential in shaping and moulding us, for better or worse as most of our mothers warned us when they suggested that we choose our friends wisely.

When I was in elementary school, I had the regular amount of friends, but there was one who was my best friend in the world. For the majority of our pre-high school years, we were inseparable, we did everything together. I know this is not uncommon, as most of us have such close, dear friends at that age. What is unique, is that looking back, we had very little in common. We lived in completely different areas of our small town. He was far more outgoing than I was. He was definitely more popular that I was. Despite my many efforts, he was more athletic than me ... but at the end of the day, none of that really mattered. We still hung out together everyday at school and made plans to meet everyday Saturday morning in the middle of that small town at the local restaurant for breakfast before biking off for the day's adventures ... of which there were many, but those are stories for another time.

As meaningful as my early friendship was, and as legendary as the sets of friends mentioned in the opening paragraph are, there is something that differentiates the deep friendship between David and Jonathan from these great examples of friendship. The bond between the king-to-be and the king's son wasn't just a connection between two individuals, but three: David, Jonathan and Yahweh.

Common ground and the cost of Friendship

We can all agree that we need friends, that those relationships are foundational in helping us become the people we want to be, and that God has created to be. I mentioned earlier that reflecting the reality of God as triune, with community at God's core is part of the need, and the gift, of having friends, and being a friend.

If it's true that we can turn to the Bible to speak to every part of our lives (and it is true!), then we can expect to find the Bible instructing us in, and confirming for us, the nature of inter-personal relationships, specifically friendships. Examining the relationship of David and Jonathan, we are given both confirmation and direction on the nature of, and building of, the friend relationship. But before we can begin to look at one of the central friendships in the pages of Bible, we need to consider who these two men are as individuals.

Lets focus first on Jonathan. We learn of Jonathan's life through the two books of the Bible that bear Samuel's name. His primary designation in Scripture, as was the norm, was to identify him in relationship to his father. Therefore, Jonathan was the eldest son of Saul. King Saul. The first king in the history of God's people, Israel. Being the first born son to the king would normally mean that Jonathan would be the successor to the throne. This fact becomes a major point in the story of Jonathan and of his friendship with David.

Much is understandably and correctly made of David's military prowess, but Jonathan was no slouch in this department, either. We first read of Jonathan in 1 Sam 13:2 and that passage recounts how he defeated a garrison of Philistines at Geba, an attack that was orchestrated with half the number of troops that his father had kept for another battle.

Following that success, Jonathan, without notifying his father, attacked a Philistine post at Micmash. Jonathan was a leader who earned the loyalty and respect of those who served with him and under him. While still in the field of battle, his father, King Saul, insisted that no one should eat anything until he avenged himself on his enemy. He actually bound his soldiers with an oath ... all unbeknown to Jonathan. After routing the Philistines, Jonathan rejoined the army and entered into a wooded area, an area in which honey was plentiful and dripping from the trees. Unaware of the oath, but hungry after battle, Jonathan reached out, tasted the honey and was immediately nourished by it. His follow soldiers were horrified and told him of the king's decree, which Jonathan immediately denounced as foolish. (1 Sam. 14:24-30)

To say King Saul was unstable is an understatement. Even though Jonathan unknowingly broke the king's oath, his father's position and piety dictated that Saul put his son to death. Intent in killing Jonathan, it was only the intervention of the other soldiers who respected Jonathan that dissuaded the king from this act of filicide.

Even before his meeting with David, we learn that Jonathan is an able warrior, more level-headed than his father the king, and he earned the trust and support of those under his command. Knowing what we know of David, is it any wonder that they became fast friends? But just in case you aren't all that familiar with David, lets do a quick recap of his story.

There are so many titles that can be attributed to David, and all of them are accurate: King, warrior, poet, musician, adulterer, murderer, but most telling, a man after God's own heart (1 Sam. 13:14).

David was the youngest son of Jesse, the great-grandson of Ruth and Boaz. When he was between the ages of 10 and 12, the prophet Samuel anoints the young shepherd as the future king of Israel. He secured a position as a minstrel for the king when his musical ability was revealed to Saul. After about three years of musical service to the king, the episode that most definitively encapsulates David's early life occurs: The confrontation with the giant, Goliath.

Israel was in the midst of its continuing warring with the Philistines. During a stand-off, with the Philistines encamped on one side of a valley, and the Israelites on the opposing hill, day after day, for 40 days, Goliath would trundle forward and bellow a challenge to the Israelites to fight with him ... and day after day, for 40 days, no one bested the giant in that challenge.

With each passing day, the Philistines grew more emboldened and continued heaping insult upon insult on God's chosen people. Until, that is, David decided that he would defend the pride of Israel and would stand tall against the towering Goliath. Once his mind was made up and he could not be talked out of the hand-to-hand confrontation, they suited the young shepherd/minstrel in the king's armour and sword.

Now to get a sense of how David looked in the king's battle gear, imagine a three-year-old boy dressed in his father's Sunday best. Nothing fit properly. David could likely barely lift the sword. He opted to leave the royal armour behind because he wasn't used to such accoutrements. Besides, David had much more effective battle weaponry - one pouch, five smooth stones, his sling and his most empowering source of strength: Going forth in the name of the Lord Almighty.

And the end result? One over-confident giant, one obedient shepherd, one well-placed stone, one giant-sized dent in the ground and the rest is history. David's reputation was set ... as was Saul's distrust and anger against David.

Clearly, David and Jonathan have military successes and the soldiering life in common, but for a friendship to grow in deep and meaningful ways, there often needs to be more than just one commonality on the table. As Scripture reveals, the friendship between these two was much more nuanced than just being "army buddies."

While entire books could be (and have been) written about the complexity and depth of this Old Testament friendship, here is a quick overview of all the other things these two had in common:

• They were both men of great faith;

• They were both men of action, eager to take the initiative;

• They were not deterred, nor discouraged by the odds being firmly against them;

• They both engendered loyalty and fierce devotion among their peers;

• The people of God loved them both dearly;

• For the most part, both men were individuals of integrity.

With all of this in common, they understood each other. With God at the centre of their existence, the soil of their lives and personalities was fertile for the growth and fruit of loving friendship that would develop between them. As they grew to know and love one another better, they likely were often amazed at the similarities in their personalities and characteristics.

C.S. Lewis, in his book on the nature of love and its expression, The Four Loves, encapsulates this well: "Friendship arises out of mere Companionship when two or more of the companions discover that they have in common some insight or interest or even taste which the others do not share and which, till that moment, each believed to be his own unique treasure (or burden). The typical expression of opening Friendship would be something like, "What? You too? I thought I was the only one. ... It is when two such persons discover one another, when, whether with immense difficulties and semi-articulate fumblings or with what would seem to us amazing and elliptical speed, they share their vision - it is then that Friendship is born. And instantly they stand together in an immense solitude."[11]

Standing together in immense solitude. Of the two of them, Jonathan must have experienced this solitude in a more profound way than David. Friendship with David meant alienation from his father. Regardless of the instability of Saul, he was still dad to David's best friend. While Jonathan regretted the king's hatred, mistrust and duplicity in dealing with David, it never impacted on his unwavering commitment to his friend. In fact, it only helped to solidify it. Their commitment to one another exceeded the bounds of camaraderie. It became a covenant.

Jonathan's commitment to this covenant is made clear in the actions recorded in 1 Sam. 18:1-4. In those verses, it says that the two friends were of one spirit, and Jonathan gave to David his robe, tunic, sword, bow and belt.

Why would he do this. Was David cold? Was the mighty giant-slaying warrior suddenly unarmed?

No. This action goes to the heart of their friendship and to the heart of all friendships: Friends are willing to sacrifice for those they call friend. Remember who Jonathan was. He was the first-born son of the king of Israel. Jonathan was the first prince of Israel. It was expected that after the reign of Saul, Jonathan would ascend to the throne. But God had a different plan ... and long before David was ready to take up the mantle of leading God's people, Jonathan coronates David by handing over to him the possessions of the next in line. He was declaring David to be the heir apparent.[12]

What a Friend We Have in Jesus

So after all the sacrifice and inter-familial tension that the relationship between Jonathan and David wrought, did they at least get to reap the benefits of best-friendship well into their senior years?

Sadly, no. Less than 10 years later, on the same day as the battlefield death of the king, Jonathan would also perish in battle, along with two of his brothers (1 Sam.31:2-3).

Why then is the story of this friendship so noteworthy among all of the Biblical stories? As Jesus is referred to in the opening line of the Gospel of Matthew as the Son of David, and as all of Scripture points us to the person and nature of Jesus Christ, there is something noteworthy in the friendship of those two men, and as the song tells us, 'What a Friend We Have in Jesus.'

What a friend, indeed!

As we read the story of this great friendship, it reveals to us many of the standards and characteristics of genuine friendship that we see fully realized in the person, life and ministry of Jesus Christ.

Real friends are one in spirit. We saw this when Jonathan gave to David his robe and weapons, symbolic of his place as the heir to the throne of Israel. It is at this point that the author of Samuel tells us that the two friends were of one spirit. When Jesus is praying for his disciples, he prays and asks of the Father "that they may all be one. As you, Father, are in me and I am in you, may they also be in us ..." (John 17:21)

Real friends love each other sacrificially and selflessly. We've already seen how Jonathan selflessly cared for his friend, but of course, the Cross of Christ is the greatest example of sacrificial love one could ever extend to a friend. "No one has greater love than this, to lay down one's life for one's friends." (John 15:13)

Real friends protect each other. Jonathan went out of his way to alert David to the plans and machinations of his father against him. In the garden of Gethsemane, on the night Jesus was arrested, tensions were high - among both those leaders and Roman soldiers who came to seize Jesus and among his disciples, especially Peter, who attempted to violently defend the Lord. Instead of allowing the situation to devolve into further violence, Jesus heals an injured servant and protects his followers by self-identifying as the one for whom they were searching. Real friends protect each other.

Real friends pursue God's will for each other. On more than one occasion we find Jonathan seeking the Lord's best - through prayer, word and action - for David. For a particularly moving example of this, read 1 Sam. 20:12-15. But in the example and life of Jesus, once again, we find this truth elevated even further. There are so many instances of this being revealed in the gospels that it is almost impossible to list them all. In a wide-angle view of Jesus's ministry, it was ALL about pursuing God's will for all people, found in His proclamation that the Kingdom of God was near. He implored people to really listen and to consider the truth of God with new commitment. Jesus' ample display of healing the ill, and exorcising evil from people restored God's will for health and wholeness to people. Individually, the restoration of Peter to the apostles' fold and the grace extended to doubting Thomas point to Jesus' pursuit of God's will in the lives of His friends.

Real friends are true to the promises they make to each other. Long after the death of his friend, David remembered their exchanges of care and support. 2 Sam. 9:1 records David asking his court, "Is there anyone still left of the house of Saul to whom I can show kindness for Jonathan's sake?" The covenant of friendship into which they entered extended beyond death. The very same is true in the case of Jesus Christ, but to the ultimate degree. Heading into the final Passover celebration and his death, Jesus predicted three times that he was about to die, but that he would be raised again to life.

The Lord Jesus is a friend of His word. Although they didn't understand what he meant, even though they forgot his promise, still some of His followers went to the tomb on that Sunday morning ... but just as He promised, the tomb was empty! He is Risen! Jesus also promised us that after His death and ascension, He would send the Counsellor to us, an Advocate, and true to His word, the Holy Spirit was sent to the Church. Real friends keep their promises.

We began this chapter with the realization that we all long to have that special friend from whom we hear, "You've got a friend in me." The good news of Jesus Christ is that in Him, each and every one of us can have that friend. In him, every one of those hallmarks of genuine friendship are found ... and they are found in such a complete manner that the word "friendship" is no longer adequate to describe the depth of caring, fulfilling relationship that He will bring to your life.

Prayer for Our Story

Gracious God, we thank you for blessing us and for keeping us.

We praise you that truly you are the God who built the reality and the beauty of friendship into the human experience. We thank you, that in consideration of your connected nature with your Son and the Holy Spirit, for building into us a longing for that connection.

We seek a better understanding of what it means to be a friend to others, and of what it means to be a friend of God. We praise you that our story is shaped by your Divine Friendship with your Creation.

Lord Jesus, You Lord, are the living sign of friendship amongst us still. When the moment of your greatest trial came, your thoughts were of us, your friends. You taught us what it means to truly be friends.

While we have never been the friend to others in the way and the manner that we should be, you have always been the Friend that you promised us that you would be. We have a lifetime of friendship with you that points us to the realities of your friendship with us.

We pray for the wisdom to recognize you as our greatest Friend, but we ask that you guard our hearts from becoming too complacent in our relationship with you, that we never take you for granted.

What a friend we have in you, Lord!

Holy Spirit, the one who is the manifestation of Christ's promise to us.

Give us the strength of Jonathan and David, to truly be a friend to those who you bring into our lives. Help us to build the attributes of genuine friendship through the set of spiritual gifts that you give to all who love you.

May we mirror the generosity of the Father in loving our friends. May we give of ourselves the way that Jesus gave of Himself for His friends.

And when we fall short of that goal, and when those we love also fail in this area, grant to us the wisdom and humility to seek, and extend, forgiveness.

Chapter 6

Can't Stand the Heat? Get into the Furnace

or

How Four Guys Show us how to Cope with Culture

(Some Chaldeans) said to King Nebuchadnezzar, "O king, live forever! You, O king, have made a decree, that everyone who hears the sound of the horn, pipe, lyre, trigon, harp, drum, and entire musical ensemble, shall fall down and worship the golden statue, and whoever does not fall down and worship shall be thrown into a furnace of blazing fire. There are certain Jews whom you have appointed over the affairs of the province of Babylon: Shadrach, Meshach, and Abednego. These pay no heed to you, O king. They do not serve your gods and they do not worship the golden statue that you have set up."

- Daniel 3:9-12, NRSV

In my experience as a believer in the life, death and resurrection of Jesus Christ, I have never faced persecution or oppression. Sure, like many of you, I've been teased, disregarded and even excluded from time to time because of my faith, but we need to be cautious when claiming powerful words like persecution and oppression.

Has the climate changed when it comes to Western society accepting those with traditional, Bible-shaped perspectives and opinions? We all know that it has ... and we know that if acceptance by the wider culture is important to you, it is becoming more difficult to identify as a Biblical Christian.

Difficult? Yes.

Impossible? No. Not at all.

We tend to reach for the stories of the well-known and famous believers who have overcome immense obstacles and challenges to their faith when it comes to this topic, but the truth is, the most convincing stories are the ones found in the faithful lives of those all around you.

But a problem arises when we realize that as we tell our stories of obedience and submission to the Lord, it often feels like we are no longer speaking the same language as those around us. We shouldn't be surprised or even dismayed by this fact, because the Bible has warned us that this is, and will be, the case. In his first letter, Peter describes Christ-followers as "aliens and strangers." (1 Peter 2:11)

It follows then that before aliens and strangers become acquainted with one another, and even after they do, it just makes sense that they speak different languages, that they have vastly different cultural experiences and expectations, and as a result of these differences, there will be some misinterpretation of intent and meanings. One only has to do a quick Internet search for language misinterpretations to see how often this happens and how humorous these mix-ups can be.

Menu translations often contain some of the funniest misinterpretations. One Norwegian cocktail lounge printed the following: "Ladies are requested not to have children in the bar." Not to be outdone, a restaurant in Vienna upped the stakes in anti-children menu translations with an item that read: "Fried milk, children sandwiches, roast cattle and boiled sheep." Almost as disturbing as the child sandwich is the idea of following it with a nice, tall glass of fried milk.

But inaccurate translations aren't always so benign and humorous. The Cold War was a dark and dangerous time, without the additional challenges of linguistic misunderstandings. At a particularly tense time during that period, Soviet Premier Nikita Khrushchev, during a speech, spoke four little words that sent a chill through the Western world: "We will bury you." Tensions quickly rose and fingers moved even closer to launching nuclear weapons, but what Khrushchev actually said in Russian was closer to "we will outlive you" or "we will live to see you buried." While the accurate translations weren't exactly sterling examples of glasnost either, they weren't nearly as stark and terrifying as the inaccurate "we will bury you."

Culture, language, economic realities, moral relativism and, of course, spiritual beliefs are all contributing factors that may make us feel like the aforementioned aliens and strangers. The translations mentioned, both the innocuous and potentially deadly, show how easily situations can escalate and be quickly twisted far beyond the original intent.

The Book of Daniel, with the namesake character and his three friends, Meshach, Shadrach and Abednego, shows us how to remain faithful when the world around us is embracing cultural and moral relativism ... and when the heat of persecution and oppression isn't just a possibility, but a crucible that must be endured.

Standing strong in challenging times

Everything about the book of Daniel makes it a story for our times. While we are aware that Scripture is written for us, but not necessarily directly to us, Daniel offers so much to the contemporary believer and reader that it is necessary to draw out some of the nuances before turning to the three friends in the oven.

In this age in which cultural connections are so very important, Daniel reflects this truth with the language in which it was written ... or more accurately, the languages. This prophetic book is written in two ancient languages, Hebrew and Aramaic. The first, introductory chapter and chapters eight though 12 were written in Hebrew and chapters two through seven were composed in Aramaic. Why the difference? Commentator Gleason Archer, Jr. surmises that the Aramaic half of the book was written addressing issues that were of interest to the entire populace of the Babylonian and Persian people, while the Hebrew section presents material directed to Jewish concerns.[13] Different languages for different cultural concerns is certainly something that is reflected in our current cultural landscape.

Also making Daniel particularly relevant to our culture is the unique nature of the book, as there are two distinct sections in the book that extend beyond just the languages in which it was written. The stories in the early chapters of Daniel are among the most regularly mined sections of Scripture for our Sunday school times, while the later parts, the prophetic apocalyptic literature of chapters seven onwards, contains some of the more difficult passages for the person in the pew.

That combination of familiar and foreign accurately mirrors how many people feel about navigating the cultural climate in which we find ourselves. Things are shifting quickly, based upon, but rapidly moving away from, their familiar foundations. To that end, we need to take a moment to consider a little more deeply the nature of this book, and why it is both familiar and foreign.

The genre of the book of Daniel is worth mentioning. Tremper Longman and Raymond Dillard point to the work of J.J. Collins in identifying the proper genre of these stories that establishes a connection to the oft-denied historicity of Daniel. Collins' own category of Court Tale captures the genre of Daniel well, and across the first six chapters, there are six episodes or stories that involve our four main characters including the fiery furnace scene.[14]

Tremper and Dillard make an important point concerning these Court Tales, and it's the main takeaway from this chapter: Daniel 3 is teaching us as God's people how to be faithful in the presence of our oppressors[15] - but again, lets be clear, many of us in the West are not oppressed or persecuted in the way that many have been oppressed or persecuted for the faith in the past, or in ways that sadly still currently occur in other parts of the non-Christian world.

But the book of Daniel points us to the victory of Christ over the world, as we learn that the faithful can make it big, even in Babylon, in places and times of oppression.[16]

So lets join the narrative of Daniel in chapters 2 and 3. This is an exile story, so we need to take a step back for some foundational information. When the Babylonian exile occurred, not all of the Hebrews were taken/forced out of Jerusalem and Judea. Primarily, the "cream of the crop," the royal court and other prominent citizens were the ones first taken into captivity in Babylon.

The first chapter of Daniel tells us that King Nebuchadnezzar commanded his staff to bring some of the more promising young exiles into the palace to be taught the language, culture and literature of the Chaldeans, with an eye towards working for the king. Daniel, and has three friends, Shadrach, Meshach and Abednego find themselves in this new training program. Daniel, after an audience with the king, pleases the monarch with an interpretation of a dream which earned Daniel a big promotion, and the king's favour. With his newfound status, Daniel also asked for promotions for his three friends, and they were appointed overseers of the affairs of the Babylonian province.

At this point, it's imperative that we make one very important point. These four young men, succeeding beyond their wildest dreams in this new, foreign land with its strange customs and ways, were able to integrate and flourish, but they never abandoned their faith in Yahweh, the God revealed to, and through, the Jewish people.

They took the First of the 10 Commandments very seriously, so they had no other god before Yahweh. They were, through and through, His people. Therefore, their success, and their faith, didn't sit well with many other Babylonians.

When the king ordered his subjects to worship a newly created statue of himself, all of the loyal (or sycophantic) officials did exactly as the king demanded. Whenever the band would strike up, all the people bowed down with foreheads on the ground before this statue. All the people that is, except for Shadrach, Meshach, and Abednego.

You know how this goes. Someone who didn't like those foreigners take all the best jobs in the palace couldn't wait to have them thrown into the fiery furnace. It didn't matter that the three didn't ask to be in the palace. It didn't matter that they were working hard to excel in their new environment. It didn't matter that they had a compelling spiritual reason not to bow before this ungodly statue.

They were disobeying, some said. They were ungrateful, others shouted. They were different, some said. Some said they had to go ... so the "loyal" Babylonians ran to the king.

A quick questioning of the three occurs, they plainly tell they king they will not worship the statue, even if it costs them their lives. But before they say anything, they offer a simple, but profound proclamation of faith.

"If our God whom we serve is able to deliver us from the furnace of the blazing fire and out of your hand, O king, let him deliver us." (Dan. 3:17).

If God is able? Every time I read that verse from Daniel, I can hear Jesus saying, as he did in Mark 9:23 to the father of the boy with the damaging spirit within him, "If I can?"

How wonderful that our God uses the very idea and language that these three young faithful men present to make his majesty, power and glory known to all in Babylon.

Outraged at the audacity of these exiles, the king orders the furnace to be heated to seven times its regular deadly temperature. He summons the very strongest of the guards to bind the exiles and to throw them into the roaring, raging furnace.

And they did. Or course, they did. The king ordered it, and so the foreigners would be tossed into the fire and burnt alive. Well, two out of three isn't bad, because as the rest of Daniel 3 reveals to us, they went into the fire, but the "being burnt alive" part didn't go quite as planned. You could say that the only thing that went up in smoke was Nebuchadnezzar's plan.

The king, eager to see his execution enacted, got as close to the fiery furnace as possible, gazed in, and through the heatwave ripples, sees not three men burning, but four, and all of them untouched and oblivious to the heat. Over the roar of the flames and furnace, the king bellows for them to come out of the furnace ... and the three step out, un-singed.

Through the Fire and the Flames

We started this chapter talking about persecution and oppression, and specifically, how most of us really have no idea what those words mean when it comes to our lives of faith. I then asked a few questions: Is it more difficult to maintain a traditional, Biblical Christianity in today's culture climate? Is it impossible to do so?

The story of Shadrach, Meshach and Abednego confirms for us that while it's difficult to do, it's not impossible. But in light of this amazing story, and the wonderful confirmation that this episode provides, answering those questions in the context of Daniel 2-3, reveals that the bar of that question is too low, it's not asking enough. Our fire-resistant exiles prove to us that we should be asking if we can maintain a Christian worldview within the climate of a blazing furnace.

And the answer to that, as the story proves, is a resounding yes!

As we navigate the fire and the flames of our current cultures, our friends-in-exile remind us of the truth of God, and the truth of our Saviour's title, Emmanuel: God is with us. If we are attentive, because our God is the same yesterday, today and tomorrow, we can extrapolate and anticipate His behaviour as we move into the challenges that 21st-century living places on our lives.

If we will stop capitulating to the demands of a morally relativistic culture, if we will stop abandoning God for acceptance by the world, and if we will cease the sacrifice of our Christian identity for some vague "spiritual awareness," we will discover (or re-discover) that we've never been alone in the first place, that truly God is with us, and we don't have to wait for the moment of conflict or trial to discern God's presence.

Imagine the shock and surprise that Nebuchadnezzar experienced when he looked into that furnace and saw not three, but four, figures there. Now double that amazement when just three step out of the fire. The king knew what he saw. He knew that four were in that space, and that one "has the appearance of a god." All of a sudden, that great statue designed to trumpet Nebuchadnezzar's might and power seemed a little silly. The king was forced to acknowledge that "there is no other god who is able to deliver in this way." (Dan. 3:29)

Nebuchadnezzar becomes aware of the great power and presence of God when he looked into the fire, but the truly encouraging aspect of this story for the believer begins with the king's initial proclamation of fiery torture.

Admittedly, that doesn't sound all that encouraging, but think back to the response of the three young foreigners. Boldly, they stand before the king and say that they trust that their God can deliver them from the flames, but even if He doesn't, they will remain faithful.

By showing up in the furnace with them, by delivering them, God has shown that he not only cares, but that He heard the proud declaration of allegiance to the Most High God, to the true King of All People. He was there! He was with them in the darkest moments. When it appeared that they were going to lose everything - position, privilege and even their very lives, God was with them in that moment. God didn't wait for the door to be closed on the furnace, He was there in the throne room, listening to the declaration of faith and fidelity.

Jesus, God-with-us, is there in every moment - strengthening, encouraging, and enabling faithful expressions of life beyond anything we ever thought possible.

How do we cope with the culture? By ensuring that our first allegiance is not to the ever-shifting trends of the day, but rooted in the unchanging, solidity of the holiness of God. Rather than alienating those around us by an unwavering faith, when accompanied by the power of the Christ-focused spiritual life, it can, and will, draw others to the truth of God.

This was not the first time that our God could be found in the fire. Moses experienced God in the flames through the burning bush. In the great appearance of the Holy Spirit, in Acts 2, tongues of fire and flame, descended upon all the believers. Our God is not only the God of wind and waves, but of fire and flame.

The church faces uncertain days ahead, and we, as believers, will face challenging days ahead, but lets learn from three young exiles, who teach us when culture turns up the heat on our faith, our God is with us.

By keeping our eyes, hearts and minds fixed on Christ, we'll never get burned by the culture.

Prayer for Our Story

Gracious God, we thank you for your blessing and for keeping us.

We praise you that truly you are the God of miracle and majesty. We recognize again that you are the Creator of all things, including the laws of science and nature, but in awe of your power, we see that you are not bound by your created laws and order.

We admit that sometimes we are intimidated by the power of the world around us. We humbly acknowledge that often we look to other sources for direction, for leadership. Forgive us in our moments of weakness, and grant to us eyes to discern you at work all around us.

We praise you, Father, as the God who is ever with us.

Lord Jesus, You Lord, are God with us. We know that as moments of pressure come upon us to acquiesce, if we rest in your strength, you are with us, now and until the end of the age.

In the dark cold of night and uncertainty, in the blazing heat of challenge and conflict, you are with us.

We pray for the wisdom to recognize you as ever-present. We ask that you guard our hearts from becoming too comfortable with being in this world. Help us to understand what it means to be in the world, but not of the world … but in all of this, never let us love your creation less, for it is formed by you, and for you, and you have sacrificed yourself for all people.

We praise you, Emmanuel, Son of God, as the God who is ever with us.

Holy Spirit, the one who is the sweet breath of God that moves among us still.

Foster in us the unwavering faith of Shadrach, Meshach and Abednego. We know that challenges and confrontations are part of the price of following our Lord Jesus. Help us to meet those challenges as faithfully as they did.

May our witness to the truth and glory of God invite others in, as Nebuchadnezzar was shown both a beautiful picture of God, and of faith in Him

May we be strengthened by Your presence in our weakness.

We praise you, Wonderful Counsellor, Holy Spirit, as the God who is ever with us.

Chapter 7

So You Can't Stand the Prime Minister/President/ Ruler/Leader

or

Praying for our Enemies/Opponents

First of all, then, I urge that supplications, prayers, intercessions, and thanksgivings be made for everyone, for kings and all who are in high positions, so that we may lead a quiet and peaceable life in all godliness and dignity. This is right and is acceptable in the sight of God our Saviour, who desires everyone to be saved and to come to the knowledge of the truth.

- 1 Tim. 2:1-4, NRSV

Let every person be subject to the governing authorities; for there is no authority except from God, and those authorities that exist have been instituted by God.

- Romans 13:1, NRSV

"Things are bad and they aren't getting better any time soon."

How's that for an encouraging start to a chapter on the importance of prayer, specifically on how crucial it is for Christ-followers to be praying for leaders of all political persuasions and stripes?

I don't remember exactly the context of when that quote was said, but I remember it being said by my then 19-year-old daughter. We were watching the news, and the American president of the day, in his crusade to make his country great again, had said, done or initiated something that, once again, seemed to divide not only the United States, but the rest of the world as well.

Not only were (and are) things bad, and not only are they not getting any better, on any given day, they actually appear to be rapidly getting worse. In preparation for this chapter, I began reflecting and asking, 'Have things always been this divided and divisive?'

The political structures of North America are inherently combative. Politicians run as much to beat the other candidate as they do to win. That may seem like the same thing, but in many cases, sadly, it is not. This may be even more apparent in the two-party system of our southern neighbours, but neither are Canadians innocent in this regard. In our parliamentary system, the party (or coalition) that comes in second in terms of voter support have a unique title: The Opposition.

And the Leader of the Opposition and her or his shadow cabinet take that role of opposition very seriously. Too seriously, as recent provincial and federal antics have revealed. All too often, every idea presented by the government of the day is opposed whether it's a good idea or not, whether it may prove beneficial to the constituency or not.

But I don't remember it always being this way. Yes, political differences have always existed. Yes, every participant wants their side to win. But, there was a level of support that previously existed that seems to have vanished as the political enterprise has become increasingly polarized. And as part of that aforementioned reflection, I think part of the reason is that the Church is not praying for our politicians, our rulers and our leaders nearly enough.

Sure, we all pray for our team, that our candidate will win, but what about after the election? When the only time that we really pay attention to the also-rans is to make sure they come by to get their lawn signs off our block. We've stopped collectively praying for all who are involved in the political process.

There are any number of reasons why this lack of prayer has insidiously wormed its way into the church, but I believe the primary reason is our fault, and it comes from one of the successful hallmarks of the current church.

I can't help but wonder if the concept of the separation of church and state has overtly and negatively affected our approach to the political process. That happens because on so many levels, a large portion of the church fundamentally misinterprets what this important idea represents. But that misunderstanding is not just in the realm of the church, the secular world also twists this idea.

The separation of church and state and the freedom of religion does not guarantee a freedom from religion. The separation of church and state was designed and implemented so that neither the state, nor the church, would have undue influence on the domain of the other. Let the church attend to the matters of the church, and the state speak to the matters of the state. Ideally, we can trace this idea all the back to the teachings of Jesus, where we read in Mark

12 that the religious leaders of the day were trying to trick Jesus into commenting on whether they should pay taxes or not.

They weren't really interested in Jesus' take on the morality of paying (or not paying) the required tax, they just wanted to twist his words to take to the Roman authorities or to reduce his influence among the Jewish people as a sympathizer with occupying Roman forces.

Seeing through the banal attempt at trickery, the Lord, in a masterful turning of the tables, asks for a coin, and asks whose inscription it bears. "The emperor's," was the reply. "Give to the emperor the things that are the emperor's, and to God the things that are God's," Jesus instructed.

Give to the state, the things of the state, and to God and God's church, the things that are God's and God's church. So what things are God's? Two come easily to mind: Prayer and people … and yes, despite the common mischaracterization of all politicians, elected officials are people, too.

Not only are they people, but they may just be among the people most in need of our prayer.

An extension of the concept

Of course, when we talk about this topic, it is readily apparent that there are extremes at either end of the spectrum. We know all too well that some political parties and their supporters have not only forgotten about the idea of church/state division, they have obliterated the concept with one becoming the extension of the other. But that's about power, not prayer.

When we are committed to keeping prayer at the core of our spiritual life, in the ways and means that Jesus modelled for us, we are not only able to pray for all people, it fundamentally changes the way that we interact with people with whom we may not agree. In this area, we can learn a lot from our Anabaptist brothers and sisters.

One such story, this one centred on an early Anabaptist leader comes to mind.

During the long, cold winter of 1569, a Dutch Anabaptist, Dirk Willems was arrested by the Roman Catholic authorities. Willems was sentenced to death by burning at the stake. His crimes? Being re-baptized and also re-baptizing other believers in his home. During his incarceration, Willems was able to escape from jail by creating a rope of knotted rags and climbing over the wall.

The Bürgermeister of Asperen in Holland, the town where all this occurred, then contracted a "thief-catcher," our version of a bounty hunter, to track down and re-capture Willems. Before long, the thief-catcher's detective skills had him on the trail of the fleeing Anabaptist, and the escape route had Willems head out across a frozen stream. The heavy-set bounty hunter hesitated to follow the fleet-footed escapee, but eventually the desire to get paid overtook his fear of thin ice.

He should have listened to his fears.

A few steps out away from the shore, the heavy man crashed through the ice and began crying out for help to the only person within earshot - the very man he was chasing, Willems. With certain freedom only a few more strides across the frozen stream ahead of him, and the flailing desperation of the drowning, would-be jailer behind him, it would be understandable if Willems struggled with the decision of whether or not to return to help the tiring, sinking man.

In the end, it was the words and teaching Jesus Christ that compelled Willems to return to the thief-catcher. With that familiar verse of Matt. 5:14 in his head and his heart, "But I say to you, love your enemies and pray for those who persecute you," Willems did exactly that. He chose to love his enemy, and returned to pull the man out of the certain icy death that awaited him.

I wish I could share that Willems' selfless, Christ-honouring decision changed that community, that the Bürgermeister relented and set Willems free, coming to a solid Anabaptist faith himself. Alas, none of that happened. The bounty hunter would have released Willems for his kindness to him, but the Bürgermeister, having heard all the commotion, had caught up with the two men by this point and he insisted on returning Willems to prison. He remained incarcerated until the day of his execution, May 16, 1569, where he was, as per his initial sentence, burned at the stake.

No one simply wakes up one morning with the spiritual maturity to risk their lives for their enemies or for their oppressors. Jesus said in John 15:18 that "no one has greater love than this, to lay down one's life for one's friends." It takes a great love to die for one's friends, but one's enemies? It's almost unthinkable. It's almost unimaginable as a first step.

But if we develop the spiritual maturity to pray for our enemies or opponents in a regular, meaningful way, the love of Christ changes that situation. No more are they simply the other, or the opponent that must be beaten, or that person that threatens my worldview. Even in our disagreements, and they can be profound, the other also remains a child of God. An image-bearer of the Most High. Someone loved by God. Someone for whom we can, and should, be praying for.

But wait, there's more: Submission and Obedience

This chapter began in the same fashion as every other chapter in this book, with the Biblical verses that are the underpinning, the foundation of each section. In the two verses that begin this chapter, we have the Apostle Paul telling us, in no uncertain terms, that we need to be praying for our leaders. Dirk Willems illustrates for us how that practice of other-focused prayer can lead to spiritual maturity with real world, hands-on application. Of course, neither Willems, nor Paul, came to these conclusions entirely on their own. As committed, faithful followers of the Lord Jesus Christ, they had example after example of Jesus doing the very things that they now challenge us to do.

Is praying for our enemies difficult? Of course it is. So then, why do it? Surely there are other avenues of spiritual development and maturity that don't require us to lift up people that we may not like or with whom we deeply disagree.

There are two ideas here that we need to consider if we are to take this "love and pray for your enemies" idea of Jesus' seriously. Not surprisingly, both of these ideas are related, and both require something of us, something that many of us are reluctant to give: Submission and obedience. There is a natural order at play here, so lets begin in order with submission.

Submission must come first in this consideration, because without it, we really aren't obeying. Sure, we may acquiesce, but that's not really the same as whole-hearted obedience. Submission has become a bit of a dirty word in our current cultural climate, primarily because the concept has been misused and abused by those who would seek to influence others or to exercise power and control over others. So to be clear, when I'm writing about submission, it's always in the context of a self-focused submission to others, not a self-desire for submission of others. That's a subtle linguistic difference, but a massive variation of application.

Through the God-inspired writings of the Apostle Paul, we are clearly called to submit to the authorities. But how can this be part of the Christian story when we see so many examples, day after day, administration after administration of politicians (of all persuasions) who are revealed to have great moral failures and whose decisions (or lack thereof) may cause real problems in the lives of ordinary people? When our primary allegiance is to Jesus Christ, the King of kings and the Lord of lords, why settle for a merely human, fallible leader?

Because God said so.

As a parent, I strived very hard during a "negotiation" with my children over chores, decisions, or activities to avoid using that development-killing phrase, "Because I said so." But there are times when it not only applies, but it applies perfectly. The good thing about answering the issue of praying for politicians, and submitting to the governing authorities and hearing, "Because God said so," is that it's not a restrictive statement, but an inclusive one. It's an invitation to grow.

The difference between God saying, "I said so" to us, and me saying the same thing to my kids, is that God never says it out of frustration. It is only and ever meant for the elevation of all involved, not to avoid an ongoing debate.

So we've clearly straddled that fine line between submission and obedience. As people of the Word, of the Christian story, whether we like it or not, we have to accept that God knows better than we do and just obey.

Because He said so. And He is God.

However, because He is the God of love as 1 John 4 clearly reveals to us, this isn't just a matter of doing what we're told because He is all-powerful, all-knowing and always right. The heart of the Lord is always with us and for us. He knows that we struggle with issues of submission and obedience ... and if we can't learn to submit ourselves and obey the authorities that we can physically see before us in the here and now, how will we ever be able to fully trust, submit to and obey the One who comes to us as the Rushing Wind and the Still, Small Voice?

In one of his more well known interactions with a questioner, in John 3:12, Jesus says to Nicodemus, "If I have told you about earthly things and you do not believe, how can you believe if I tell you about heavenly things?" Again, we can extrapolate a current context application out of Jesus direction to the Pharisees. If we can't submit and obey to the God-ordained leaders that we see (and that we often get to vote for), how will we ever get to the point of submission to God?

This call to submission and obedience is just as much for us as for the leaders in question. We can never forget that our great God, the author of the story of life, is concerned for all of us.

There is of course, one final reason to pray for our politicians and it's this: They need to be uplifted more than they need to be thrown under the bus of public opinion. If you've ever complained about our civic leaders (and lets be honest, who hasn't), the gift of prayer is just that - a gift that is meant to be shared. If our prayer lives are focused solely on our own wants and needs, that's not genuine prayer as much as it is demanding intervention to give us what we want, when we want it, and how we want it.

And that certainly is not the model of prayer that we receive from the Lord Jesus.

As we read our Bibles, and reacquaint ourselves with the Story of God, we encounter a long list of kings and leaders who benefited greatly by the prayers of the prophets and the people, resulting in blessings for all involved.

Sadly, the list is even longer of all the politicians and royal leaders who did not value prayer, nor did they receive any prayers on their behalf, and the pages of Scripture are full of the sadness and calamity that arose as a result.

So, as with all things with God, when we submit, when we obey, it benefits us, and it benefits others.

Prayer for Our Story

Gracious God, we thank you that many of us have a voice in selecting those who rule over us.

We praise you for the great and wonderful example you set for all the leaders of the world. In you, we find justice and fairness, we see provision and consideration. As you are the very source of love and mercy, we see that reflected in all of your decisions and in the way you have lead all people since the moment of their Creation.

Again Father, we admit that sometimes we are intimidated by the power of the world around us. We humbly acknowledge that we often look to other sources for direction, for leadership other than those that you have ordained to lead. Help us to trust, submit and obey. Help us to choose our leaders wisely, discerning your will in all matters.

We praise you, Father, as the God who leads like none other.

Lord Jesus, You Lord, are God with us. In you, we find the perfect examples of submission and obedience. Taking fleshly form through your Incarnation, you laid aside your rightful position as Creator and Sustainer, and subjected your Glorious Nature to the confines of human experience.

We marvel at how difficult it must have been to allow yourself to be mistreated, abused and murdered by the officials and leaders of the day. Through every encounter you model for us the example of obedience to the entire Word and Plan of the Father.

May we be inspired by your devotion, and your commitment to the Higher Things, the Things Above, not the things of this world.

Holy Spirit, we long for your gentle guidance, your ever-present counsel and enlightenment in dealing with both our earthly leaders and Heavenly King.

We admit that we bristle when forced to submit ourselves to the wills of others, especially those with whom we often disagree. But in this prayer, we affirm the words of the Apostle Paul. By the inspired Word of God, we will offer supplications, prayers, intercessions and thanksgiving for all in authority.

We pray that you might continue to move through them, calling them to a deeper well of wisdom, a Christ-focused approach to leading.

Gentle Spirit, we pray that you would grant to us strength to elevate the other. We pray for discernment, and we pray for hearts and minds that are committed to offering the very best of what God has graced us with for the betterment of all around us.

May we be strengthened by Your presence in our weakness.

We praise you, Wonderful Counsellor, Holy Spirit, as the God who is ever with us.

Chapter 8

The Screenplay Gospel
or
Why Mark's Gospel is So Important

Now John was clothed with camel's hair, with a leather belt around his waist, and he ate locusts and wild honey. He proclaimed, "The one who is more powerful than I is coming after me; I am not worthy to stoop down and untie the thong of his sandals. I have baptized you with water; but he will baptize you with the Holy Spirit."

In those days Jesus came from Nazareth of Galilee and was baptized by John in the Jordan.

- Mark 1:6-9, NRSV

Long before I took the truths of Christianity seriously, I had a connection, an affinity, for Mark. I wish that I could share that my rapport with the gospel of Mark was due to its ability to spark a deep, theological awakening within my restless spirit ... but the truth is that my connection to the book was nothing nearly that profound: My appreciation for Mark grew out of my laziness as a young man.

As a child, I was raised in the Roman Catholic tradition, and as such, I attended Roman Catholic, separate schools. One of the strengths of that school system is that it integrates the life of faith into the daily education of its students. As an adult, there are reasons why I no longer worship within a Roman Catholic liturgy and context, but I remain grateful for the basic foundations of the Biblical story which were imparted to me during that time. Years later, when I was in crisis, those Scriptural truths and stories came bubbling to the surface from deep within, sustaining me and enabling me to reach out for help.

But back to my Catholic school days. As part of the aforementioned school/faith integration, there was a focus on preparing students for the sacraments and the rites. First Communion, First Confession and Confirmation were big deals and major events in the life of Catholic faith and in the school year. A large part of the religion classes for the school year in which I was confirmed were subsumed by the preparation for the Confirmation event.

Again, let me remind you that I was far more interested in the things that occupy the mind of a young boy, including hockey, friends, comic books, and girls, than in the rich tradition of Confirmation. Part of the Confirmation preparation was to prepare a stole that was to be worn over the confirmation gown.

The stoles were to be adorned with a few appropriate religious symbols, and most importantly, the confirmation candidate's newly chosen confirmation name.

The letters and symbols were to be drawn on felt, cut out and sown onto the stole, all done by the student as a way of preparing and contemplating on the serious nature of the Confirmation sacrament. Friends were choosing names like Bartholomew and Zechariah. As you've probably guessed, I settled quickly and early on for the name Mark. Not because of the content of his gospel or the role he played in the early church, but because his name was only four letters long, which meant far less time working with felt, and more time after school working on my wrist shot (which needed the work … and still does).

It was also suggested by both our teacher and the attending priest that we should know as much as possible about the Biblical person from whom we would take our confirmation name. In addition to having only a few letters to manipulate out of felt, the gospel of Mark has the fewest chapters of all the gospels. Being the briefest of all the accounts of Jesus' life was a major factor in my decision, much to my shame.

Much later, as I came to know Jesus as Lord and Saviour, I would develop a deep love for the gospel bearing Mark's name. Of all the people highlighted in the Bible, outside of the Lord Jesus, I love and connect with Peter most clearly.

When I discovered that the Gospel of Mark was the record of Peter's memories and teaching of Jesus, the second gospel immediately became a favourite of mine … for many reasons, some theological and some from a writer's perspective. The next few chapters will explore Peter and Mark's theology through some wonderful stories, so in this chapter we will look at Mark's gospel and the story of Mark's book.

Mark - the person

Before we can take a good look at the story of Mark's gospel, it's imperative that we take a moment to consider Mark, the person. While all of the gospels reflect the intent and purpose of the author, they also reveal a little of the character and personality of the writer. Considering how foundational the Gospel of Mark is, not only to the entire canon of Scripture, but also its profound influence on the other synoptic gospels (Matthew and Luke), we serve the story of the gospel well by contemplating the one it was named after.

So then, who was Mark? Well, for starters, he is known through the book of Acts, by a similar, but different name, John Mark. I suspect that part of the relationship and affection that Peter may have had for young John Mark was a similarity in their respective beginnings in ministry. Like Peter, Mark had what could be called an inauspicious start in ministry, abandoning Paul during his first missionary trip.

The majority of Biblical scholars today agree (though not unanimously) that the John Mark of the Book of Acts is Mark, the gospel writer. Also widely accepted is the understanding that Mark is the same young man associated with Peter in the earliest traditions of the church.[17] So what does the Book of Acts tell us of John Mark?

One of the first things that we learn is that his connection with Peter was established early in the history of the church. When Peter is released from prison in Acts 12:12, where does the apostle go? To the home of Mark's mother. Clearly a follower of The Way, as a believer, she welcomed Peter into their home.

Later in that same chapter of Acts, we read that John Mark accompanied Paul and Barnabas (who was Mark's cousin), on their return trip to Antioch from the Holy City. Jumping ahead to Acts 13, John Mark is listed as a helper for Paul and Barnabas during the first missionary journey. What Mark's ministry duties were on this missionary initiative are unclear, but as Walter Wessel comments, "Whatever its nature, it brought him into close relationship with Paul and Barnabas."[18]

However, John Mark's status as missionary helper was short-lived. During their work in Perga, Pamphylia, Mark felt the draw back to Jerusalem and so he left the duo of missionaries for the safety of mom's house. While we don't know for sure why John Mark felt it necessary to leave, historians and commentators do offer a few possible scenarios. It is suggested that Mark may have been uncomfortable with Paul assuming a greater role and becoming the focal point over his cousin, Barnabas. Another interesting possibility is that like Peter, John Mark was initially uncertain of, and even reluctant to, taking the Good News of Christ to the Gentiles. While there is no definitive proof of this, it would help to explain the warm relationship between Peter and Mark.

Also like Peter, John Mark would eventually resolve any theological restrictions on sharing the truth of Jesus with the Gentiles. Unfortunately, that theological and mission-minded clarity didn't come quickly enough for Paul. When Barnabas suggested including John Mark on the proposed second missionary journey, Paul steadfastly refused to allow the young man to join the mission. That refusal led to the dissolution of the missionary partnership as we read in Acts 15:36-39. From there, Barnabas and

Mark set sail for Cyprus, and we read no more of Barnabas nor John Mark in the Book of Acts.

Thankfully, we read later in the epistles of Paul that reconciliation between the two men did occur (perhaps due to Mark overcoming his reluctance to minister to Gentiles), and we have a few occasions of Paul mentioning and commending Mark in his writings. John Mark is included in Paul's letter from Rome to the church at Colossae: "If he comes to you, welcome him." (Col. 4:10) Wessel suggests that it is at this point that John Mark was beginning to ingratiate himself back into Paul's favour.[19] As the story of Paul unfolds through Acts, the church epistles and the pastoral letters, we learn that by the end of Paul's story, the two men had completely reunited, leaving former squabbles behind them for the sake of the church and to honour the Lord. Writing again from Rome, Paul wrote to Timothy that he should "get Mark and bring him with you because he is helpful to me in my ministry." (2 Tim. 4:11) Of course, with the deep bond between Peter and Mark continuing to develop, it's not surprising that we also read from Peter in the conclusion to his first letter that he shares greetings from Mark, whom he affectionately calls "my son." (1 Peter 5:13)

What I didn't know when I chose Mark for my Confirmation name was that while he had a short name, and the shortest gospel, he had a big, big story ... with a big faith to match. That big story and faith would propel his gospel of Jesus Christ into one of the most important documents in history!

Mark - the gospel

In the introduction to his commentary on the Gospel of Mark, David Garland reveals that the outline to the gospel is found in the most successful sermon every preached. The Apostle Peter addressing the ever-growing Pentecost crowd of Jews in Jerusalem, found the crowd curious to learn of God's most recent display of his power and grace, and he declared that the Holy Spirit had been gifted to them by God, thereby inaugurating a new age for humanity. Acts 2 records Peter's sermon in full, but it is in verses 22-24 that we are presented with the outline for Mark's gospel.[20]

In that section of his sermon, Peter calls the crowd to recognize a few things: That Jesus of Nazareth, by the power of God performed miracles, signs and wonders among the people; that Jesus was handed over to the people with the foreknowledge and permission of the Father; that by the intent of "wicked men," Jesus was killed by being nailed to the cross, but by the great love and abounding grace of the Father, Christ was raised from the dead, leaving the spectre of death behind, because death could not hold him, his love for the world was too great!

This is the outline for the gospel, but the magnificent way Mark presents the Christ story from Peter's recollections and teachings, coupled with the "behind the scenes" information that only Peter could provide, makes the gospel not only a fascinating read, but truly transformative ... for those who would have ears to hear.

Although Mark is the second gospel presented in the New Testament, it was the first written, and therefore the oldest of the four gospel accounts of Jesus' life. When Mark sat down to put Peter's thoughts and lessons about the Lord down for others to benefit from, I often wonder if he was aware that he was creating an entire new genre of writing in the gospel.

I mentioned the outline to the gospel in the introduction to this section. Lets now draw a distinction between the outline and the structure, and when I use the word "structure," I am referring to the style of writing that Mark employs in his writing. I've had the privilege of preaching through the Gospel of Mark a few times, and I love doing so. It's such a fascinating read and the style is perfect for preaching. And why is that? Mark is what I've often called "The Screenplay Gospel."

The writing in Mark is so active, so kinetic. From the opening verses of Chapter 1, which skips over genealogies or birth stories, it propels, it drives the reader full-speed-ahead through 16 chapters to the Empty Tomb and the Easter miracle. From the first words, it has the end in sight. Buckle up, because Mark is revealing the promise of Messiah right out of the gate.

Chapter 1, verse 1 says this: "The beginning of the good news of Jesus Christ, the Son of God." From our comfortable chairs, padded pews and relatively safe and easy lives, those are familiar and comforting words. But 2,000 years ago in the Near East of Israel, those words are anything but comforting. Those are fighting words ... and so the Screenplay Gospel begins.

Clearly, by my use of the term "Screenplay Gospel," I find there to be a very cinematic aspect to the gospel presentation. There are many filmed versions of different gospels. Some are good, some are great and some, well, some are not so great, but to my knowledge there has only been one filmed version of Mark's work, but the propulsive narrative style that Mark employs cries out for more exploration.

Mark's main focus for writing the gospel is to portray the Lord Jesus as the Suffering Servant-Saviour. His main, first audience was the Gentile church in Rome.[21] In an effort to make that case, Mark's focus is on the serving **work** of Jesus. This is a servant who is busy, always busy, doing the work of the Father ... even in times of rest and contemplation, there is intent and purpose. Every step, story, healing and miracle reveals the truth that the Kingdom of God is near.

Mark captures this sense of propulsion and activity so well with the language he chooses and utilizes. As Hughes writes, "Christ is all action in Mark."[22] Throughout the gospel, the writer uses the word 'immediately' 42 times across the 16 chapters. Just for comparison with the other synoptic gospels, that's six times as many uses as occur in Matthew, and 42 times more frequent than in the Gospel of Luke. The episode, teaching or healing occurs, Mark yells "Cut" on the scene and immediately presents the next scene to his followers.

The descriptions of the events that Mark records are verb-driven. Jesus is busy doing all the things that the Son of God must be about during his time in earthly ministry, so we have Jesus healing, teaching, walking, arguing, exorcising demons and loving the people ... all the time in the present tense. Not only is he busy, but he is engaged in his activity. Jesus is not just going through the motions, but he is setting up the next scene, moving ever closer to the climax of the screenplay ... I mean, the gospel.

When we consider that Peter was the main source and resource for Mark's writing, the sense of urgency that jumps off the page when we read Mark shouldn't come as a surprise to us. In Peter, we have a man who was also "on the go." Peter was a man of action, even if that action occasionally created trouble for himself. Nonetheless, Peter was never afraid to take that first step out of the boat.

Mark's presentation of Jesus as the Suffering Servant-Saviour so hit the mark that both Luke and Matthew would use Mark as the template for their gospel accounts of the Lord Jesus' life. Mark's systematic account of the ministry and life of Jesus was so captivating for the first readers that the other synoptic writers would include all of Mark's narrative, save a very few words.

Like a skilled director, Mark is able to see the big picture and deftly captures the gospel story of Jesus, as presented through Peter, creating a fascinating, compelling and life-changing true story. Equally engrossing is the subtext to the gospel story, being the story of Mark himself. From his early days as a weak-willed, uncommitted follower of Jesus to his elevation as one of the key figures of the Early Church, a rock-solid disciple of the Lord, biographer and eventual martyr, Mark's story, and his world-changing gospel are both profoundly important for Christ-followers today.

Prayer for Our Story

Gracious God, we thank you for the truth that you continue to choose all sorts of people to serve you. We thank you for the truth that you don't always just call the qualified, but you always qualify the called. We see this in the life of John Mark.

So, dear Father, we praise you for your wonderful patience. We praise You, for truly You are a kind and benevolent parent, nurturing us, cultivating those gifts that you have planted in our personalities, gifts that we often don't see, won't see or are undisciplined enough not to develop.

We thank you that the with-God life is not stagnant and dull, but as the writing of John Mark reveals to us again, life with You is vibrant and active, kinetic and energetic. May our daily walk with you reflect this truth, and may the energy which is Yours be made known in us, so that we might share Your presence with others.

We praise you, Father, as the God who is the source and inspiration of all life.

Lord Jesus, You are the Suffering Servant-Saviour. In page after page, episode after episode in Mark's account of your blessed life, we read of you serving in every possible way: Teaching, loving, healing, combatting evil and following the lead of Your Father as the inspiration of all life.

At this point in our journey through these pages, it is appropriate to thank You and praise You for Your role as Saviour. You are not merely another godly servant, You are Messiah. You are the Son of God.

We praise You, because truly, You are the Alpha and the Omega, the beginning and the end. You defeated death, meaning Your great Love for the Father and for all humanity could not be denied. It was too great to be contained by the grave.

We praise You as Saviour, and we model our lives on You as Servant. We love you because You are Lord!

Holy Spirit, we look at the life of John Mark, and we see Your gentle encouragement, and perhaps Your forceful direction. We see a life changed by the love of the Father, the life of the Son, and Your presence, sweet Spirit.

So, we too, pray for transformation. We each have areas of weakness. Like Mark, perhaps we are slow to accept the truths of God, perhaps we are headstrong, unwilling or unable to follow those that You have installed in positions of authority and leadership.

Grant to us the servanthood trait that our Lord Jesus so clearly demonstrated on the pages of Mark's gospel. Like Peter, help us to be sensitive to the move and activity of God all around us.

We praise you, Wonderful Counsellor, Holy Spirit, as the God who is ever with us - inspiring us to be more than we are today, and trusting that You are not nearly done working in us.

Chapter 9

Unintentional Streaking
or
Worth Losing your Pants Over

Then Jesus said to them, "Have you come out with swords and clubs to arrest me as though I were a bandit? Day after day I was with you in the temple teaching, and you did not arrest me. But let the scriptures be fulfilled."

All of them deserted him and fled.

A certain young man was following him, wearing nothing but a linen cloth. They caught hold of him, but he left the linen cloth and ran off naked.

- Mark 14:48-52, NRSV

Having established that the Gospel of Mark really is the Screenplay Gospel, I'm going to ask you to think back to some of your favourite movies.

Before you get to the climax of the film, whether it's the long-awaited kiss between the leads in the movie, the big battle scene where the heroes finally defeat the forces of evil or when the lead investigator secures the one missing piece of evidence that guarantees a conviction of that smug career criminal, before any of those great moments occur, there is usually one very important scene or moment that enables the emotional climax of the moment to have a deeper resonance.

In 'Star Wars: A New Hope,' before the tie-fighters are dispatched on the potentially suicidal attack on the Death Star, it's the bonding that takes place between Han Solo and Luke Skywalker, only to have that new friendship strained by the poorly timed departure of the bounty hunter and the Wookie.

In the Jimmy Stewart seasonal classic, 'It's a Wonderful Life,' long before the Bailey front room is flooded with the townsfolk of Bedford Falls pitching in to save their good friend George from financial ruin and jail, there are several of those "pointing toward the end" moments. The brilliance of the director Frank Capra in presenting disappointment followed by bright spots in George's life, and repeating the pattern through the entire film until the insurmountable disappointment occurs … insurmountable, that is, until the angel Clarence shows up.

'The Godfather' has one of the most definitive pre-climax set-up moments in all of film. The returning war-hero, Michael Corleone, wants nothing to do with the family business, as the family business is organized crime. But an attempt on his father's life, which reveals not only the corruption of the other mob families, but of the evil to be found in the "civilian" world of politics and law enforcement forces Michael to reconsider. This begins a series of events that takes years to unfold, but eventually, Michael is no longer referred to as the war hero, but as Don Corleone.

All of these scenarios draw us deeper into the narrative, the emotional payoff of the story. And the Gospel of Mark is no different ... except, of course, that John Mark the Evangelist isn't just writing or directing a popcorn flick, he is sharing not only the greatest story ever told, but also, the truest story ever told.

To Have Been There

As mentioned in the previous chapter, by language and intent, Mark is focused on presenting readers with the picture of Jesus as the Suffering Servant-Saviour. He does this with examples of action. In the Gospel of Mark, the evangelist is committed to showing Jesus about the work of the Father. As such, there is a real kinetic feel to the gospel. When read in one sitting (which only takes a few hours - I heartily recommend doing so), you get a different sense of the earliest written gospel. It bristles with energy, moving the reader quickly to Mark's highest focus, the Cross, the Crucifixion and the Resurrection. All are dealt with matter-of-factly, maintaining the break-neck pace of the established narrative.

But before we get to those important events in chapters 15 and 16 of John Mark's writing, we have the aforementioned key development moment, that incident or series of moments that reframe everything that is to follow, and actually allows the climax of the story to begin. In Mark, we have that event in Chapter 14, and in typically Markan fashion, it is at turns beautiful and horrific, forward moving but encapsulating everything that has come before.

For me, this is a marvel of writing. Somehow, John Mark is able to step outside of his usually propulsive writing style in the latter part of Chapter 14. While there is no reduction on the sheer volume of activity, somehow the Evangelist is able to write it in slow motion. If this section of the gospel were filmed, it would have been done at half-speed. Every movement, every word, every single breath is seemingly accounted for and marvellously highlighted. As we will discover in a few moments, this detail and colour that John Mark brings to this particular episode, and the evening in question, is not just due to Peter's accurate retelling of the event. If it seems like this level of interaction with, and recording of, the events of the Gethsemane garden could only be offered by an eyewitness, by someone who had lived through the events, that is because many commentators believe that John Mark was just such a witness - he was there with Peter and Jesus that night!

One of the highlights and key theological moments of all the gospels is the institution of the Lord's Supper. That final Passover meal in which Jesus explains, in words that are repeated by faithful congregations to this very day, that the Passover was all about Him. "This is my body ... this is my blood ... take and eat." The betrayer is revealed, the end game is set in motion. Jesus comforts his friends, they pray, they eat, they sing.

Tradition tells us that this momental episode of human history occurred in the upper room of John Mark's mother's home, which had become a popular, important place in the formation of Jesus' followers.[23] Having occurred in his very own house, it is not difficult to imagine young Mark listening at the door, peeking in to see the itinerant rabbi that everyone in the city was buzzing about. After the meal, they sang the traditional Passover hymn, the second part of the Hallel, from psalms 115-118. Why does Mark include this detail? Again, this speaks to his masterful presentation of the unfolding events. Recognizing that his first audience would have been intimately aware of the Passover traditions (certainly much more familiar than the church today), the sung portions of the Hallel would have reminded his audience that Jesus headed "into the Gethsemane garden and its agony with such promises as follows:"[24]

"The Lord is my strength and my song;
he has become my salvation.

Shouts of joy and victory
resound in the tents of the righteous"
'The Lord's right hand has done mighty things!
The Lord's right hand is lifted high;
the Lord's right hand has done mighty things!'

I will not die but live,
and will proclaim what the Lord has done."
(Psalm 118:14-17)

Imagine hearing the deep, resonant voices of Jesus and the 11 disciples as they sang these words before heading off into the night to pray in the garden. Wouldn't you want to follow along with them? Of course you would ... and Mark certainly would, because tradition suggests that is exactly what he did. In fact, he was so intent on following the Lord and the disciples, that Mark didn't even stop to ensure that he was fully dressed.

As Wessel explains, the normal clothing style for men of this time was a two-garment combination. The undergarment was known as the *chiton*, but the young man in the garden was only wearing the *sindon*, the outer garment.[25] Young John Mark, after peering in on the upper room activity for a while, had perhaps retired for the evening, when he heard Jesus and the others leaving. Eager to catch up to them, perhaps he just changed into his *sindon* so as to not waste time.

When things devolved into chaos in the garden and the guards started grabbing everyone, someone got a handful of the young man's *sindon*, but determined to get away, Mark twisted his way out of the outer garment. While he was free, he was left to flee back to his home naked.

As mentioned earlier, the unfolding events of chapters 14 and 15 are among the most dramatic recorded not only in this gospel, but in the entirety of Scripture. So then, with the weight and importance of this story, why would Mark choose to include this somewhat extraneous detail in the narrative?

We turn to that answer in the next section.

Keep your pants on

The post-Passover hymn is finished. Jesus and the disciples arrive at the Gethsemane garden and he instructs his followers to remain just inside the garden gate and pray. He then takes the inner circle of friends, James, John and Peter, with him deeper into the grove to join him as he prays. They all promptly fall asleep and Jesus tries to revive them three times, urging them not to miss this crucial moment of prayer with him, but alas, that moment has passed.

Judas, the betrayer, arrives with soldiers and the unruly crowd, and chaos shatters the serenity and silence of the garden. Betrayal, confusion, and violence are the result of the confrontation. We read that all of Jesus' followers and friends abandon him, with special attention given to the one young man who is forced to flee, leaving his expensive, linen *sindon* behind him.

So, again, why is this detail so important to John Mark that it warranted its inclusion? There two reasons, one theological and one stylistic, so lets deal with the 'lighter,' style reason first. Remember, we've been referring to the Gospel of Mark as 'The Screenplay Gospel.' A common technique utilized by many film directors is to insert themselves into their films in background roles. The filmmaker most famous for doing this was Alfred Hitchcock. The master of suspense can be seen during 40 scenes of his remaining 54 major films. Many other directors have followed Hitch onto the silver screen in cameos, including Steven Spielberg, Peter Jackson, Ron Howard, John Hughes and directing legends John Huston and Cecil B. DeMille.

Perhaps they all got the idea from John Mark, because many feel that the Evangelist wrote of his own Gethsemane experience, and that he was the young streaker from the garden. I suspect that this is true, and that Mark was indeed in the garden following the disciples that night. His presence would account for the different tone to chapter 14 - he wasn't relying solely on Peter's account, he was an eyewitness for these events.

But Mark isn't nearly so self-centred that he would write himself into the account just to draw attention to himself. I'm certain that the Evangelist replayed that night over and over again in his mind's eye, and when the Holy Spirit prompted his crafting of Peter's story of Jesus, that night featured large in the theology that Mark was revealing.

The first thing that his *au naturel* escape into the darkness says to us is that those followers who loved the Lord were desperate to get away from him ... at any cost! What did this mean for Jesus? It meant that he was about to face his darkest night, the trial and the cross entirely and completely alone. With no earthly friend in his corner, without even a modicum of human comfort or support. Entirely alone.

Other commentators suggest that there is another foreshadowing at work here. By inserting the fact that the outer linen garment, the *sindon* was left behind, it points us to the tomb. Jesus body was prepared for burial by being wrapped in a linen cloth (Mark 15:46), and the women who attend the tomb on Sunday morning were greeted by a young man in a white robe who imparts the news of the resurrection.[26]

Considering all that Mark gained as a result of having the *sindon* literally torn off his back, perhaps it was worth losing his pants over. Despite the initial embarrassment, the brush with the authorities that night and the years of self-questioning that likely followed the garden episode, Mark was never the same.

For us in the 21st century, we are still called to leave everything behind, but unlike Mark, we don't leave it all behind to get AWAY from Jesus, but to get closer to him. The Lord is quite clear in his call to all people, we must be willing to sacrifice everything for him - family, friends, ambitions, finances, opinions. To be worthy of him, we must be entirely his.

It's fitting that Jesus calls us to be born again. In John 3:3, the Lord Jesus says: "Very truly, I tell you, no one can see the kingdom of God without being born from above." Of course, each of us comes into the world the very same way, and that's the same way that Mark leaves Gethsemane: naked.

During those times in ministry with Paul and Barnabas, when John Mark's enthusiasm and commitment to the work of Christ wavered, on the long journey back from the mission field to his mother's house, I'm sure he remembered the long, naked, journey back to his mother's house from the garden the night Jesus was arrested.

Sometimes being born (again) is a longer process for some. The labour is intense, difficult and painful. Mark's late-night clothesless sprint isn't just a vanity note in his gospel writing, it was a clarion call for each and every one of us to consider the cost of following Jesus. It was a reminder and a warning that if we truly want to see the coming of the kingdom of God, we will gladly leave everything behind.

Prayer for Our Story

Gracious God, the ever-present, loving Father,

We pray for the strength to turn to you when situations are bearing down on us,

And for the strength to always pursue your will in the darkest nights.

Lord Jesus, the One who faced that long, dark night of the tormented soul,

We pray for forgiveness, because like your friends and the young man in linen,

All too often, we have turned and run, leaving you behind. Forgive us, Lord.

Holy Spirit, the One who knows our weakness,

We pray for the strength to stand firm in our convictions

And for the ability to overcome our desire to run when things get difficult.

Chapter 10

The Days of Wine and Withered Fig Trees *or* *Failing to deliver on promises*

Seeing in the distance a fig tree in leaf, (Jesus) went to see whether perhaps he would find anything on it. When he came to it, he found nothing but leaves, for it was not the season for figs. He said to it, "May no one ever eat fruit from you again." And his disciples heard it.

In the morning as they passed by, they saw the fig tree withered away to its roots. Then Peter remembered and said to him, "Rabbi, look! The fig tree that you cursed has withered."

Jesus answered them, "Have faith in God."

- Mark 11:13-14;20-22, NRSV

I like to cook. I'm not a great cook, certainly not Masterchef level, but I enjoy putting meals together for our family … and no one has expired from food poisoning, so I guess I've been doing something right. Well, most of the time, at least.

While I delight in culinary pursuits, that does not extend to baking. I may have moderate meal skills, but I have next-to-zero baking ability. May I tell you a story?

A number of years ago, when our children were very young, for some reason, I got it into my head that I should bake a cake for my beautiful wife. Perhaps it was her birthday, or our anniversary. Neither of us can remember the details. In fact, the whole cake fiasco was so awful that my wife has completely erased the ordeal from her memory. It's probably better that way (but I suspect she's just being kind).

I'm not sure where I went wrong. It may have been too much of an ingredient, but more likely I neglected to include all of the required components. However, whatever I did put in the mixing bowl was well mixed, poured into the baking pans and baked at the correct temperature for the appropriate amount of time, and when I removed it from the oven, it looked great.

I allowed it to cool, also for the appropriate amount of time, and then when it was cool enough, I began the decorating phase. Remember that this was an event cake, so I wanted it to look great. I carefully applied the first layer of frosting, and then let it set for a few moments.

Next, I applied the icing flourishes to make the dessert as sugary-perfect as I possibly could. I don't mind sharing (and you'll read why in a few sentences), that the cake looked fantastic. It was bakery-store-window amazing. I had never created anything in the kitchen that ever looked remotely this good. I was so proud, and so eager to get through dinner just to present the celebratory cake that I remember giving everyone smaller portions of the main meal, so that they wouldn't be too full for dessert.

The moment had arrived! I presented the cake to my wife and she commented on how wonderful it looked, and it really did look great! She cut into it, served up four slices of the cake and I sat back intent on taking in the joy of my family as they tasted what would surely be the best dessert they had ever eaten, but to my utter surprise, it was not to be.

My family certainly all had expressive looks on the faces, but it was not the expression that I was anticipating … or that I ever want to see again. To put it bluntly, the cake was awful. As wonderful as it looked was inversely tied to how bad it tasted. I've had a mouthful of sand that tasted better than this cake (but that's a story for another time).

When something looks the way that it is supposed to appear, or if it looks even better, we expect that whatever is contained within will be equally as good. This is the situation that we have here in Mark 11 and the encounter with Jesus and the fig tree.

When is a fig tree not a fig tree?

This episode from Mark contains all of the previous, wonderful screenplay qualities that we've mentioned in the preceding chapters. There is motion, purpose and interesting events. Travelling from Bethany, the time on the road has made the Lord Jesus hungry. Looking down the road, perhaps to see how much farther they have to travel to get back to Jerusalem, he sees a fig tree in the distance.

The fig tree is described as being in leaf, meaning that it was in full bloom. Even though Mark tells us the agricultural truth that the tree was not ready to grow figs just yet, the tree had caught the attention of the Lord because of its abundant foliage, but when he inspected the tree, there were no figs to be found. The attractive leaves failed to deliver on the promise of tasty fruit.

Back to my doomed dessert for a moment: All the icing in the world could not have saved that aforementioned, ingredient-deficient cake.

Like the fig leaves, the frosting promised something good to eat, but it did not deliver.

What happens next has been a subject of discussion among theologians for some time. Not having the figs that he was expecting, Jesus curses the tree, causing it to wither from the roots, never to produce fruit ever again. Some commentators have called the actions of Jesus into question here. Why would he do this, they ask. It wasn't even the season for figs yet, therefore the tree did nothing wrong. Among the more bold criticisms are to call Jesus petulant and petty. William Barclay has written that "the story doesn't seem worthy of Jesus. There seems to be a petulance about it."[27]

After accusing Jesus Christ, the One who is both truly God and truly human, of petulance we need to examine if that is what Mark is actually recording for us in his gospel. Consider all that we know of Jesus. Think of his tender interactions with the sick and broken. Review the heated, but loving, interactions with the religious rulers of the day. Reflect on the few warranted expressions of his holy anger at the cheapening of the sacred things of God. Does 'petulant' sound like an apt description of the Messiah?

Our interpretation of one's acts must line up with the facts on record.

I love the music of John Coltrane. It is my opinion that his masterwork from 1964, A Love Supreme, is one of the most beautiful pieces of music ever conceived and recorded. Now that you know those facts about me, is it likely that I would ever destroy a vinyl copy of that great record just because the album cover was defaced or torn?

You can deduce from the facts presented that I would not. Surely then, from the truths presented, from the entirety of Scripture, we can discern that Jesus' response here is not one of petty, temper-tantrum lashing out. So then, we have to ask another question: What is the story here?

It's imperative to note that this weird encounter with the fig tree sandwiches another trip from Bethany into Jerusalem. Jesus' triumphal entry into the Holy City had just occurred the day before, and the echoes of the shouts of Hosanna still lingered in the hearts of those who loved the Lord. The fig tree wasn't cursed because Jesus was 'hangry' - food is not the issue here. Jesus is giving his disciples, and through Mark's writing, the Lord gives to all of us, a visual parable of what was happening in Israel,[28] and by extension, what may be happening to us. It's also a parable of the danger of fruitlessness in the lives of God's people.

On the way into Jerusalem, Jesus curses the tree. When they arrive in the Holy City, Mark records the shambles that the Lord finds the temple in. Once again, Jesus is forced to drive out the money changers from the house of prayer. He did so three years earlier when he began his ministry, and once again he is forced to do so, to repeat that clearing action. To convey how seriously Jesus considered the money changers transgressions against the intent of the temple, in the original language, Mark uses the same phrasing for "driving out" as he does when he is describing exorcisms. But it's not just those making profit off the faithful with whom Jesus is angry. His righteous anger also burned against those who were buying, as well as those who were using the temple courts as a shortcut through the city, a practice prohibited by the Mishnah (the first written collection of the Jewish oral traditions). In short, the temple area, instead of being the house of prayer that Isaiah and Jeremiah[29] wrote about, it had become a chaotic, noisy desecration of the holiest site in Israel.

Mark shares that as evening fell, the Lord and the disciples left the city to return to Bethany. I imagine the journey back to Bethany must have seemed twice as long, with heavy, broken hearts as a result of the Temple encounter. The following morning provides the other part of the visual parable sandwich as the travellers once again approach the fig tree, and appropriately, it's Peter who draws the dying, withered state of the tree to their attention.

The real-life parable centres on being fruitful, and we'll unpack that in the next section, but Jesus' response to Peter is beautiful and encouraging. Still dismayed over the heart-breaking state of the Temple, he doesn't even mention the fruitfulness aspect to his teaching, but stresses the importance and the power of prayer.

Do you see the connection between fruitful, spiritual living and healthy prayer?

Too many non-fig trees, not enough wine

Many prophets, including Jeremiah, Joel, Micah and Hosea, have utilized the image of the fig tree to represent Israel in their prophecies and writing. The fig tree in Mark 11, with all of the outward signs of growth, health and vitality, but without one single edible fig, perfectly reflects what Jesus witnessed at the Temple. It was a beautiful structure teeming with life, but was actually dead inside. As a result, as Hughes suggests, Jesus actually ends up blessing the tree with that curse, making it the most famous fig tree in history, calling countless thousands to examine their own lives for signs of fruitfulness.[30]

The question we need to ask ourselves after the fig tree story is, of course, are there genuine signs of life in our spiritual lives? Behind the outward displays of church involvement, a perception of holiness in your circles, are you bearing the fruit of faithfully following Christ? That question is not posed judgmentally, as I know that it sounds harsh, but in light of fig tree parable, our Teacher has not left us room to whitewash or downplay this question.

In giving the parable of the fig tree, Jesus says clearly that just because we may look good on the outside, if we aren't bearing spiritual fruit, we can expect to be dealt with harshly. Mark is thorough in his description of the cursed tree, highlighting that it had withered down to its roots. Why does that matter? It indicates that the righteous judgement of Christ on the tree was whole and absolute. The destruction was total.

While Jesus is unequivocal in his treatment of the tree, as I mentioned earlier, we must look at all the evidence that Scripture gives to us in the forming of our opinions on people and situations. Yes, Jesus is acting in accordance with his previously revealed calls to holiness and his high regard for the holy places and institutions of the Father, but he is also gracious and forgiving. As that is true, this fig tree story always brings to mind another story, the story of the first miracle recorded in the Gospel of John: The wine at the wedding in Cana.

The second chapter of John contains the first account of Jesus driving the money changers out of the Temple court. This account has the Lord fashioning a whip out of cords, then he forcefully drives those away who would defile the holy place. Immediately before those episodes are two wonderful connections to the second Temple clearing in Mark. First, at the end of John 1, we are introduced to the disciple Nathaniel (also known as Bartholomew), and where do find him? Jesus sees him beneath a fig tree, and says with the image of Israel over Nathaniel, "that he is an Israelite in whom there is no deceit." Jesus recognizes the outward and the inward signs of healthy spiritual life in Nathaniel.

Then we come to one of Jesus' most well-known miracles, the water into wine. Perhaps because of the Nathaniel/fig tree connection, these two events are forever linked in my mind ... and in my life as I continue to follow Christ.

The wonderful thing about this miracle is that it is completely unnecessary. Yes, it saved the wedding couple and the families some embarrassment over running out of wine, but despite the popular phrase, it is unlikely that anyone actually dies of embarrassment. This was just a wonderful display of the abundant love and great generosity of God. This is a joyful proclamation that Jesus Christ's ministry has begun.

For us, as we look at the Mark 11 and John 1 and 2 combination of passages, we learn that God cares deeply for our spiritual practices. It matters that the things of God matter to us, and if they don't matter to us, if we don't display the fruit of spiritual growth in our lives, there are consequences ... but if we do take this seriously, the blessings of God are rich, full and oft-times, entirely unexpected.

So, take stock of your spiritual "fig trees." If you find genuine fruit of the Spirit among the cultural and religious leaves of our lives, drink of the wine the Lord provides and rejoice! However, if you neglect to find any fruit, let me encourage you to re-read the story of your life and find where you lost the plot.

Prayer for Our Story

Gracious God, the ever-present, loving Father

We praise You for your righteousness and Your holiness, for inspiring prophets and poets to share your nature with the world.

You, Father, are Other and Everywhere, may we find you in all places.

Lord Jesus, the One who loves the Holiness of God like no other,

We pray again for forgiveness, because like those in the Temple courts, we all too often take the things and presence of God for granted.

May you open our eyes to the importance of the Sacred. Forgive us, Lord.

Holy Spirit, the One who exists in perpetual Sacredness,

Move our hearts and souls to long for a true appreciation of the Holy,

And nurture in us soil in which the spiritual fruit of God may flourish and grow.

Chapter 11

Rash Decisions Rarely Pan Out

or

How Confidence can Peter out

Again (Jesus) asked them, "Whom are you looking for?" And they said, "Jesus of Nazareth." Jesus answered, "I told you that I am he. So if you are looking for me, let these men go." This was to fulfill the word that he had spoken, "I did not lose a single one of those whom you gave me." Then Simon Peter, who had a sword, drew it, struck the high priest's slave, and cut off his right ear. The slave's name was Malchus. Jesus said to Peter, "Put your sword back into its sheath. Am I not to drink the cup that the Father has given me?"

- John 18:7-11, NRSV

Peter said to him, "Even though I must die with you, I will not deny you."

- Matthew 26:35, NRSV

"Lord, if it's you," Peter replied, "tell me to come to you on the water."

"Come," he said.

- John 14:28-29

I share the following story to my own great shame. Let me be clear, I'm not retelling this story in an attempt to amuse or to justify the behaviour that I'm about to describe. Quite the opposite in fact, I'm sharing this story as one of the many regrets that I have, but also with the grateful understanding that the good Lord has forgiven me for such foolishness.

During my high school days, I was fortunate enough to make the junior boys soccer team. I write "make the team," but I think everyone who tried out for the squad was allowed to play. As my school was in a more rural part of the province, we often had to travel by bus to play teams at schools out of our region. To reduce the travel costs, the high school league often arranged for the junior and senior teams to play on the same afternoon, allowing the teams to travel together, requiring only one trip instead of two.

Following one such outing, as the bus travelled through the city to reach the highway, you can imagine the conversation and antics of a busload of high school energy and testosterone. Somewhere along the way, some of the senior players began shouting out the bus windows at any woman unfortunate enough to have been on the route we were travelling. Following the lame attempt to gain female attention and approval, the teams would then "rate" this person on the famous one-to-ten scale.

Eager to fit in with the older players, I began to look ahead for any female form while the debate raged in the bus over the best-looking women on the trip. After a few blocks of surveying, as we approached another female pedestrian, I was able to shout out something like, "Here's another babe coming up!"

It's actually surprising that we didn't tip the bus over as every player plastered themselves against the windows on one side of the bus to see the woman that I had pointed out. As we drove by, the woman would not have been described as a supermodel, and she was probably about 70 years old … at least she appeared so to my 15-year-old self.

You can imagine the reaction of the other players on the bus. Needless to say, none of the comments that were hurled at this poor woman - or at me - are suitable to print here. Nor did I make any inroads that night with the senior boys team. It was a long, silent ride home for me that night. To my greater shame, it wasn't until much later that I realized that my initial response to what had occurred had little or no consideration for what that woman must have felt, I selfishly focused on just how embarrassed I was.

My regret all these years later is not that my taste in women was questioned for the next three years of high school, but that I ever felt that it was acceptable to judge anyone that way, and that I sought to curry favour with the older players by belittling another person. I won't try to explain away my poor behaviour by saying I was just a dumb teenager (although I was) or that "it was a different time." Every time is a different time, and what is unacceptable is unacceptable regardless of the year on the calendar.

This was a classic case of "Shoulda, Coulda, Woulda."

I should have never objectified another person and just kept my big mouth shut.

I could have made a better choice.

I would learn, as I often do, the hard way.

But thankfully, I did learn how incredibly inappropriate this entire scenario was … and as I moved out of my teenage years, I quickly learned that I wasn't alone in making poor, rash decisions. In fact, our Bibles are full of people who also make dumb mistakes, and sometimes they make more than just one of them. Amazingly, the God of the Universe continues to love and use those blunder-making people over and over again. When I began to read the Bible seriously, I immediately found a kindred spirit in Peter. Not to be flippant regarding his status in the canon of faith heroes, but Peter could be described as the Patron Saint of Shoulda, Coulda, Woulda.

No wonder I love him so much.

And then Jesus shows up: Think, act, repeat.

Peter's story offers so much to believers today. As Jesus knew what was in the hearts of all people, I believe that Peter's unique personality and potential for real, genuine spiritual growth is the reason that he was chosen, and why he was part of the Lord's "inner circle." As we look at some aspects of Peter's story and seek to apply it to our lives today, we'll focus on how Peter teaches us to think before we act or speak, and finally, and perhaps most importantly, how to deal with the self-esteem issues that plague so many of us.

Before we get to those important elements of Simon Peter's story, lets take a moment to reacquaint ourselves with the great apostle and pillar of the early church. Let's begin with his name as he is known by several through the Biblical texts. He is referred to, in different places as Peter, Simon bar Jonah, Simeon, Cephas and Rock. Let's begin with the variations of Simon. Peter's birth name was Simeon, which as a result of anglicizing, through the English translations of the Bible, became Simon. The book of Matthew tells us that Simon was the son of Jonah, which is where we get the Hebrew phrase 'bar Jonah', 'bar' meaning 'son of.' Being an Aramaic-speaking, first-century Galilean meant that Simeon would likely have been known as Shimon. That name, Shimon, is a derivative of the Hebrew word 'shema,' which means 'to hear' or 'to listen.'[31] Immediately, the etymology of the names in Peter's family let us know that there is something wonderful and unique happening here. How fitting it is that Shimon would be among the first to hear and listen to Jesus as he begins his ministry.

Now consider the family business.

Peter, his brother, Andrew, and his father were fishermen. I love that the fisherman father of Peter is named after Jonah, who, the Bible tells us also knew a thing or two about fish himself.

As far as manual labour goes, it doesn't get more intense than the work of a first-century fisherman. In addition to the strength it must have required to throw out the heavy nets, and to haul the soaked, (hopefully) fish-laden nets back into the boat, fishermen also had to contend with the elements: The blistering sun, the bleaching salt of the sea, the forceful winds, the driving rain. The life of a fisherman was not idyllic, but hard, difficult work.

These were men shaped by a hard world and a hard day's work. I imagine that the average Galilean fisherman did not suffer fools gladly. They were men of action, solid, dependable as the day is long. They were men who took pride in their work, their family and their names … and then Jesus shows up and before long, Shimon is no longer used, Simon is briefly used, and Jesus begins changing the son of Jonah, beginning with his name. He is now Peter, or Cephas in Greek, which means Rock, and we'll discuss that in the last section of this chapter.

One of the most endearing truths about Peter was his impulse to action. When a situation occurred, his life-long conditioning out on the fishing boats meant he was trained to react. Peter's life revolved around situations arising, action taken, issue resolved. Stopping to think out on the seas might mean the loss of a net, meaning the day's wages, and the replacement costs, were lost. Conditioned, reflex responses were the order of the day ... and then Jesus shows up.

From the very beginning of their journey together, Jesus challenges Peter's approach to, and understanding of, life. The immediate response is no longer always the appropriate reaction. Peter is forced to reassess his understanding and response to God, to religion and to who constitutes the people of God.

His story is beautiful because it is a real story, the kind of story that reflects most of our lives, with successes and failures, taking one step forward and two steps back. This is made most clear on the night that Jesus was arrested in the garden of Gethsemane.

After being invited to join the Lord for a time of prayer and reflection, what does Peter (and James and John) do? They fall asleep. Not once, but three times. Then the Roman guards and Jewish officials arrive to arrest Jesus. The Lord, true to nature, steps up and tries to diffuse the situation by identifying himself and asking for conversation. Peter, also true to nature, grabs the first sword available, and starts swinging at the heads of the intruding crowd.

It is literally by the grace of God that the only victim, Malchus, the high priest's servant only lost an ear. The story would have had a very different ending if Peter was arrested for murder that night. Again, his actions in the garden indicate a reflexive response to the situation at hand, and we must remember that this incident happens after three years of day-to-day contact with Jesus. Imagine how impulsive Simon Peter might have been before he listened and heard the truth of God through Jesus.

But Jesus isn't done with Peter yet. Even with the unfolding events and their consequences on, and for, Peter, the Spirit of God would continue to mould him and shape him from the impetuous, impulsive, act-first, think-later person we have in the gospels to the mature, thoughtful leader that the early church would need in Acts.

And to think that Jesus saw all of this in Shimon when he called him to follow him, with the promise that he would become a fisher of men. (Matt. 4:19)

Think, think again, then speak.

For Peter, it wasn't just his impulsive actions that often lead him into trouble, his tongue was also a major contributing partner in his problems. While Peter had to learn how to think first and act only afterwards, he also had to learn the discipline of thinking first, and then, and only then, opening his mouth.

This is part of the reason that I have such love and affinity for Peter, as this is something with which I can relate. I wonder how much different my high school sports life would have been without the incident that opened this chapter. I also often wonder if that episode had any lingering effects on the poor, innocent woman who just happened to be in the wrong place as our bus rolled by. I sincerely hope she was able to dismiss the entire exchange as being from the shallow minds and characters of a busload of teenage meatheads.

Like Peter, I have suffered from enough foot-in-mouth situations, that I know full well the unpleasant taste of shoe leather, followed by an ample helping of crow. While they often go hand-in-hand, they really don't complement each other very well, and both leave a lingering, nasty aftertaste.

There are a few episodes of Peter speaking before thinking that we could highlight here, including the offer to build dwellings on

Mount Tabor for Jesus, Moses and Elijah after the Lord's Transfiguration (Mark 9:5). He is quickly informed by the Father's voice that he should just pay attention to Jesus and listen to him. Had he not spoken in that moment, who knows what he may have witnessed or heard. This would have been a perfect time for him to revert to Shimon, listening and hearing.

Another of Peter's cringe-inducing inappropriate comments is recorded in Matthew 16:22-23. The Lord Jesus had been revealing to the disciples his sacrificial plan for salvation that included surrendering to the authorities and being killed, but conquering death three days later, to be resurrected by the Father. There are a few understandable responses to this revelation: Perhaps quietly going away to reflect on the deep theological consequence of what Jesus had shared; taking a few moments to consider what impact this would have on the burgeoning ministry that you had been a part of for years; even wondering if Jesus had lost his mind would be an comprehensible reaction.

As we know, Peter opted for none of the above. Jesus shares what will be shortly coming, and Peter's rejoinder is take the Lord aside, and begin harshly chastising him, saying that this must never come to pass. Peter, in the heat of the moment, was blinded by his love for Jesus, and actually spoke against the very will of God. Without thinking about it, he was willing to condemn the rest of the world to judgement and death, removing the only acceptable method of salvation and atonement for the sin of the world.

That may be the most theologically egregious speaking blunder, but the most painful one to read, is not surprisingly, one of the most well-known stories about Peter. On the night when he was betrayed by Judas, mere hours before he was arrested, Jesus told Peter that before the night was over, Peter would deny him three times. Of course, Peter doesn't take the time to contemplate why Jesus would say such a thing, after all, Peter was part of the inner circle of disciples. He had been earmarked for leadership, but it never crosses his mind to address why Jesus would say this.

Nor does Peter ask why the Lord has prophesied in this way. No, instead Peter's initial response is an emphatic one: Even if I must die, I will never denounce you. (Matt. 26:35) Of course, he does deny the Lord three times just as Jesus said he would, and knew he would.

Here, Peter's inability to think before he speaks is revealed as the damaging trait that it has always been. Our words and the way that we express ourselves has real-world consequences. Peter's hastily uttered and emphatic rebuttal to Jesus is more than just another embarrassing slip of the tongue, it's an utter failure of character ... and sadly, this is why so many of us relate to Peter.

We're more than just our mistakes

Having spent the majority of this chapter denouncing Peter for acting and speaking without thinking, I need to restore a little balance to the equation. Another reason that I love Peter is because through the Biblical narrative arc of Peter's life and ministry we do see real, God-inspired growth and maturity. From the rough and tumble fisherman of the gospels to the mature, inclusive leader in Acts to the church elder and statesman that are portrayed through his letters, Peter is a study in the practical growth of a Christ-focused follower.

Part of that narrative arc, as I mentioned earlier, is the one-step forward, two-steps back nature of Peter's life. But on one occasion, his impulsive nature resulted in a two-steps forward, only one-step back situation ... and making these steps especially noteworthy is the fact that they occur on the surface of the sea!

When we read of Peter's brief water walk in Matthew 14, there are a few noteworthy items for consideration that will factor into the storm scenario. Chapter 14 opens with the death of John the Baptist, someone that they all knew. Following the news of the prophet's death, we have the feeding of the 5,000 event. Miracles and death are clearly on the minds of the disciples as Jesus makes them get into the boat without him and begin sailing across the Sea of Galilee.

As they were navigating the night-time crossing, a storm blows up. As the disciples are fighting the wind and the waves, with heads still swimming with details of John's death and the miracle of thousands fed from so little, another seemingly supernatural event occurs: There appears to be someone - or something - walking towards them across the waves.

Understandably, those in the boat are more than a little frightened by this, and they began screaming for help. Hearing their cries, the Lord eases their concern by saying, "Ego eimi," translated as 'It is I." This immediately soothes the worried minds of the disciples, and why? Part of the answer is found in Jesus' response. 'Ego eimi' would bring to mind the phrase "I am," which is how God identified himself in the Old Testament.[32]

But Peter again responds quickly without considering the full, imparted truth of Jesus' words. Peter says, "If it is you, command me to come to you on the water."

And Jesus does.

And Peter steps over the side of the boat.

And by the power and the word of Christ, the disciple doesn't sink to the bottom of the sea, but actually joins the Lord in the supernatural stroll across the waves and whitecaps ... until he starts to think, until his mental processes overpower his faith in Jesus, and perhaps he thinks something along the lines of "What am I doing out here? I can't walk on water." When he thinks that, when he considers that he is out there under his own power, and not the power of God in Jesus, he's correct: He can't do it and then he begins to sink.

Before his faith and confidence petered out, for those first, fledgling baby steps, Peter displays the faith that he would later come to possess more fully. Making this even more impressive is the truth that Peter should sunk like a stone, or a Rock.

As mentioned above Peter was named the Rock, and he earned his new name when Jesus asked the disciples what the people were saying about Jesus. Who was he? After a few answers, he asked them who they thought Jesus was.

Guess who answered first? No sooner had Jesus posed the question, Peter speaks up with his Galilean fisherman's voice, "You are the Messiah, the Son of the Living God." (Matt. 16:16). Peter's rush to answer without thinking, served him well in this instance. His answer not only earned him a blessing from Jesus, but he provided the foundation for the development of the Christian church: The bold proclamation that Jesus is the Messiah; the truth that Jesus is the begotten Son of the Living God is the central truth to the person of Christ.

Vocalizing this enables the understanding of everything else to follow: The miracles to come, the Last Supper, the death and Resurrection and the formation of the church.

Peter shows us again and again, that even when we say the wrong thing, that even when take our eyes off the Lord and start to sink, even when we resort to self-damaging first impulses, we're more than just our mistakes.

We are beloved children of God, daughters and sons of the King. So, as long as we continue to express the truth, as Peter did, that Jesus is the Son of God, and the light and the hope of the world, He will continue to build His church in us, and through us.

Prayer for Our Story

Gracious God, the ever-present, loving Father.

We praise you for your loving ability to call all people to Your purposes, whether we are fishermen, doctors, store clerks or politicians. We are all your children, and for that we love you as Father.

You, Great God, are the architect of a mighty faith that strengthens the weak, and weakens the strong!

Lord Jesus, the One who sees beyond our limitations and struggles to find something worthy of loving in each of us,

We praise you for being not only the God of Salvation and Rescue, but being the God of friendship, the One who still calls to broken people like us, 'Follow Me.'

May you open our eyes to our deep need for friendship and relationship with you.

Holy Spirit, the One who lifts us beyond our fears and second guessing,

We know that you are able to make much of our efforts to serve the Lord God. Like you did with Peter, we pray that you would magnify our humble efforts of faith and service to share your great truth with the world around us.

May we be open to the great possibilities that exist in life with You.

Chapter 12

The Same Sun that Melts the Wax, Hardens Clay
or
Why some believe and some don't

And he told them many things in parables, saying: "Listen! A sower went out to sow. And as he sowed, some seeds fell on the path, and the birds came and ate them up. Other seeds fell on rocky ground, where they did not have much soil, and they sprang up quickly, since they had no depth of soil.

- Matthew 13:3-5, NRSV

Why do some people turn out the way that they do? Why will two people, presented with similar choices and opportunities make radically different decisions and choose vastly different paths. Is it just a matter of preference and personality or is it about discipline and willingness?

Some of the most compelling stories are about siblings or close friends who opt for different life experiences. These tales are so entertaining they have almost become stereotypical tropes in our culture: The clergyman/gangster brothers; the lawyer/thief combination and the good girl/wild child pair of sisters. Holmes and Moriarty have long typified this other side of the coin device, as have Frodo and Gollum.

There, but for the grace of God, go you and I.

We began this book looking at perhaps the most famous, and the most concerning of all these types of stories: Cain and Abel. They were of the first entirely naturally born generation of God's people. A mere one generation removed from the supernatural creation of God's people, and they exhibited profoundly different choices.

Can we blame it on the expulsion from the Garden of Eden? Were the effects of the Fall that immediately devastating on the souls and lives of those within the fallout zone of that first sinful choice? We may never know the answers to those questions on this side of heaven, but we do the following truths: Both Cain and Abel were loved by their parents; they were both loved by God; they both literally had the entire world before them; despite their common upbringing, they chose different professions. Cain was a farmer, working the ground and Abel was a shepherd, his trade was livestock.

Perhaps the biggest, obvious difference between the first brothers is evident when we look at their faith. In the story of what led to their separation, we read in Genesis 4 that God preferred Abel's offering over Cain's. This wasn't a case of the Father preferring a burger over a salad, but of God preferring the intent from which the offering was made. Abel's offering was made in faith, giving the best of his flock, the firstborn, as a sacrifice to God. Cain, on the other hand, offered almost as an afterthought "some" of his produce as his offering.

There is nothing in the Genesis account to indicate that one of the brothers had curried more favour with God before the offering story. Cain and Abel had equal access and standing before the Lord prior to the tragic unfolding of their story. It boggles the mind how it could have gone so wrong, so quickly.

Equal opportunity. Equivalent access. Vastly different results.

Sometimes, as the old saying goes, the same sun that melts the wax hardens the clay.

The power of parable

It is inevitable that when writing a book about the importance of story, and the beauty, wonder and applicability of the Biblical stories that we focus on Jesus, the master storyteller himself. Even among those who don't recognize the divinity of Jesus Christ, he is constantly upheld as a story-based teacher without peer. So many of the Lord's stories have become foundational parts of our culture. The Good Samaritan, the Prodigal Son, the House built on Sand - all of these teachings have extended beyond the margins of the church and believers' lives into the wider culture. So then, we are forced to ask, why is that true?

The answer lies not in just one area, but a combination of answers that speak to the unique nature of the storyteller himself. Jesus utilized stories in his teaching to great effect because of the content, the perspective, and his own divine nature. The stories were relevant to the audience. They were informed by a greater awareness than just the typical Near Eastern worldview, and because Jesus is God Incarnate, they were saturated with God's holiness.

Of all the different techniques of story-based teaching that Jesus employed, he is most well-known for the parable. A parable is often a deceptively simple story that is used to illustrate a complex moral or spiritual lesson. It's no surprise then, that Jesus, as the source of all spiritual truth would be such a master in taking intricate spiritual and theological concepts and making them digestible by framing them in commonplace, understandable situations.

Among the aforementioned great and well-known parables of Jesus is the exemplum of the Sower and the Seed. It is recorded in all three of the synoptic gospels, not recorded only in the Gospel of John, which contained none of Jesus' parables. This lesson answers that question of why some come to faith, and others do not.

Here's a synopsis of the story from Matthew 13: A farmer goes out to sow his seed. As he scatters the seed, some landed on the pathway and birds swooped down and ate it. Other seed fell on rocky places without much soil. The seed grew quickly because the soil was shallow, but the sun scorched the plant without the protection of the soil, causing the plant to wither due to the lack of roots. Another grouping of seed landed among the thorns, which grew up and choked out the plant. But one section of the scattered seed landed in good soil, where it produced a bountiful crop, yielding an unexpected, generous harvest.

So then, we are given four different scenarios for the seed to grow: The pathway, in shallow soil, among the thorns, and the good soil. Regardless of where the seed fell, both the seed and the sower are the same for each situation. Therefore, we can easily deduce two things: The focus of the parable is not the sower, but the soils, and in each instance the sower has done the same amount of work. No soil received preferential treatment.[33] Although we have four different growth successes and failures, what is never questioned is the quality of the seed, nor the work of the farmer.

We are fortunate that with this parable, at the request of the disciples, Jesus takes the time to explain what the parable meant - something that Jesus rarely does. He was usually content to let the story stand and let time, reflection and spiritual development occur to reveal the truth and meaning of the parable. But this time, Jesus speaks into the story behind the parable.

But before he does so in Matt. 13:18, there is a command to be heeded. Jesus commands the disciples to listen. Theologian D.A. Carson suggests that the original Greek language is emphatic, as many have longed for deeper explanation, Jesus is saying, I'm sharing this with you, so YOU listen!

The seed is the good news about the Kingdom of God. Our spiritual enemy, lack of discipline, a shortage of commitment, love for the things of the world are all given as the reasons for the challenges to good growth in the soil of the human heart and soul.

So with the focus then on the condition of the soils and not the sower nor the seed, we begin to see why this story still resonates today, perhaps even more so than when the Lord originally shared this story.

Becoming 'roots communities'

As we begin to reflect on the current application for the church and for individual believers in our current context, before we move to the soils of people's lives, we must not exclude the role of the sower. While the sower is not the focal point of Jesus' story, we err if we skip too quickly to an outward focus of this story. We must consider our role in the contemporary consideration of this parable.

Our responsibility is to ensure that the Good News of the Kingdom seed continues to be sown. If Carson is correct and Christ spoke emphatically to his disciples that they must listen to his explanation, I will follow the Lord's lead and emphatically stress that all believers are responsible for sowing that seed of evangelism. Who knows? It may be the Spirit of God working through your voice and personality that aids in the transformation of soil from unreceptive to welcoming.

Given then, that we all have equal access to the truth of the Kingdom of God, Jesus tells us why one brother's gift is acceptable and other's is not, why one sibling chooses a life of crime and another dedicates their life to service to God through the clergy. The reasons listed earlier in this chapter - love of the world, lack of personal commitment and discipline to the Christian faith and our spiritual enemy, Satan - these obstacles to knowing, and choosing God have never found more receptive soil than that of the late 20th and early 21st century, and there are many reasons for that, including the wealth of life in the West, the proliferation of alternative spiritualities and the claim to no spirituality, and of course, the presence of our spiritual enemy. I'm not one to look for the Devil around every corner, nor am I prone to blaming the Liar for every calamity that befalls us, but in this case, I have to take the damaging presence of Satan seriously, because Jesus takes it seriously.

The first reason that the Lord gives to us for those not being able to grow in the faith is that the Devil snatches their joy away. I'm sure that if you have journeyed with Jesus for more than 10 minutes you have seen this played out in your own life and the lives of other believers. Doesn't it always seem to be the case that when the Kingdom of God breaks through the haze of everyday life, when we start really living for God and the Kingdom, that all hell breaks loose (literally) in almost every area of our lives? Without being rooted in something deeper and truer, is it any wonder that people would abandon this seemingly trouble-filled way of life?

Our church guests books are filled with the names of people who have come into our church halls, get connected with a few people, make an initial impact on the faith community … and they end up breaking the pastor's heart because a short time later, they fade away. The joy that they exhibit at the possibility of a deeper connection with God through the Holy Spirit burns brightly at first, but burns out all too quickly.

Perhaps the saddest of all the soil scenarios is the one that Jesus explains next. A person, weighed down by the cares, concerns and worries of the world, actually hears the good news of the Kingdom of God, but they are so invested in the world and its systems, that they are incapable of responding appropriately to the lifeline that has just been thrown to them. A quick survey of the daily news on any given day provides enough evidence that the ways of the world are claiming too many innocent lives, destroying families and shattering dreams … and for what? More money? Increased influence and power? How this must break the heart of our Great

God as He has made all the things that truly matter available to us through Christ.

But it's not enough for us who know the truth of this story to merely say, "They have made their own choice. Now they have to deal with the consequences ... but we'll pray for them." In each one of the scenarios listed above, the church has a role to play. We need to ensure that our faith communities are roots builders. We need to regularly be working the soil to enable the seed of God's Kingdom not only to be planted, but to flourish and grow into something beautiful.

Our story must be one in which we are unwilling to lose one more person to the machinations of our enemy. We must be a place where we model, by word and deed, the truth that life with God is more beautiful and meaningful than the size of our bank accounts or anything that we can order from Amazon. We must be willing to invest in, and invite, newcomers to our faith lives in such a way that they also want their roots to be driving deep through the soil of their hearts into a new water source, the Living Water that only Jesus can provide.

As Christ's people in the world today, the Holy Spirit can use us to help determine whether some stories end with melted wax or hardened clay.

Prayer for Our Story

Gracious God, the ever-present, loving Father.

We praise you for revealing your Kingdom to us, through your Son, your Spirit, your prophets, your Word and through the believers that you have placed all around us.

You, Great God, are the One who still wins over hearts to this very day. May it always be so. May your Glory and Love be more prevalent in all of our lives.

Lord Jesus, the One who is the Way, the Truth and the Life, you are also the Master Storyteller.

So we praise you for the loving, but firm, way that you have revealed the deeper things of the Kingdom to us. May we always have the desire to search your words and your teaching for the full meaning that you want us to discover.

May you open our eyes, our hearts and our souls to the deep truth in all of your teaching.

Holy Spirit, the One who illuminates our hearts and our minds,

We know that we have been in that place where the truth of the Son was either going to melt the wax in our lives, or harden our hearts towards God. How can we ever thank you enough for drawing us closer to the Son?

May we be open to your move within our lives, and ever open to the deep and abiding truths of God.

Chapter 13

Love Wins
or
The Importance of the Cross

"If you keep my commandments, you will abide in my love, just as I have kept my Father's commandments and abide in his love. I have said these things to you so that my joy may be in you, and that your joy may be complete.

"This is my commandment, that you love one another as I have loved you. No one has greater love than this, to lay down one's life for one's friends. You are my friends if you do what I command you."

- John 15:10-14, NRSV

Several times throughout this book, I've intentionally used the phrase, 'the greatest story ever told.' The Bible stories that we've looked at so far are all individual pieces of the larger, greater narrative that constitutes our Scriptures, and as a whole, it is absolutely the greatest story ever told.

But now we need to add another word to that apt description, because not only is it the greatest story ever told, it's the greatest LOVE story ever told.

I know as I share that with you that it is a big, bold claim. Anytime we use the word 'greatest' in relation to anything, especially in these post-modern days when absolutes are viewed as exclusionary and non-valid, it immediately opens up room for disagreement and pushback.

I'll prove that now, using examples of films, but I'll need your help. Very quickly, think of what you consider to be the best love story movie of all time.

Depending on your particular vintage, you may have thought of Casablanca. If you're a little younger than that, perhaps the love story movie, Love Story, was the one you picked. If you were an '80s kid, there's a good chance that Say Anything is your choice. Feel free to add your choice to these: Love Actually, An Affair to Remember or The Notebook.

It doesn't really matter which one you chose, because I'm going to disagree with you. The greatest movie love story of all time is The Philadelphia Story, starring the two greatest stars of Hollywood's Golden Age (and my two favourite actors), Katharine Hepburn and Jimmy Stewart ... Cary Grant is also in it, and I suppose he does a good enough job. But for me, it's Hepburn and Stewart that carry the film, even if theirs isn't the main romance in the film. This film has everything: Commentary on the differences between the sexes, between the classes, inter-familial tension and conflict, snappy pacing and witty dialogue … and did I mention Hepburn and Stewart?

You see the manner in which we choose these things is always subjective: Our personal tastes, our ages, our relationship status will all impact how we answer a question such is this. Which is why we need to have a more definitive criteria for deciding what is the greatest love story of all.

And that's the reason I feel most comfortable with stating that the 'greatest love story ever told' tag is not earned by comparing it to other love stories in our culture, but by a higher standard. In fact, it's the highest standard of all, the very book we've been discussing all this time, the Word of God.

It turns out that the disciple John, the follower described as the one whom Jesus loved, has a lot to say about the topic of love.

In the 15th chapter of his gospel, he records Jesus issuing this commandment to his followers: That they love each other as Jesus has loved them.

That's a pretty high bar, a lofty standard for which to aim in our relationships, but Jesus doesn't stop there. In fact, he raises the stakes even higher.

In the very next sentence, verse 13, the Lord says this: "No one has greater love than this, to lay down one's life for one's friends."

Therefore, we can safely, accurately and confidently say that the Bible is the greatest love story ever told, because Jesus did exactly that: He laid down His life for you!

Even though this chapter has had a light-hearted introduction, the love story that we are now turning our attention to is anything but flippant. Love is serious business.

The Look of Love

There are dozens of versions of the classic song by that name, and many other different songs with the same title. But what does love really look like?

It looks like a cross. It looks exactly like a man, who was so much more than just a man, stretched out upon that cross. Many have said this looks like defeat and failure, but it was the exact opposite: The cross looks like victory and love. It is the ultimate symbol of the central truth of God - God is love, and love wins!

I will suggest that the cross is the second most important symbol in the Christian faith. The only more significant symbol in the faith is that of the Empty Tomb ... but we can't get to the miraculous truth of Easter Sunday morning without the darkness of Good Friday and the Cross. As we highlight the importance of the cross and the Lord's crucifixion, it is imperative that we address some of the issues expressed by many concerning the Lord's death.

My use of the word 'issues' in the previous sentence could easily have been 'misunderstandings' to be polite or 'intentional mischaracterization' in some cases. Few realities of our faith draw more criticism than the truth of the cross, so lets address a few of those misplaced remonstrances.

The death of Jesus Christ is one of the most divisive components of the Christian faith. Those who question whether Jesus really was God Incarnate, frequently ask the question, 'If Jesus was God, how could he have been killed?' Unfortunately, this question, and those who pose it, are coming to the question from the wrong direction. Jesus' death was not something that happened to him without his awareness, rather it was the entire point of his life - to provide the sacrificial atonement that would provide the way for a fallen world to regain the deepest fellowship with the Father. The cross didn't happen to Jesus, the Saviour was born for the cross.

The common rejoinder to this claim is that it's just revisionist history, that believers say these things to make the best of a bad situation or to try to rationalize, or explain away how things went so horribly awry. The problem with this perspective is that we have so much Scriptural evidence from the story of God to dispute that attempt to minimize the claim that Jesus was always headed towards the Cross. In Peter's first letter, the apostle writes that we were ransomed from our futile ways, inherited from our ancestors, not by passing items like silver and gold, but by the precious blood of Christ, like that of a perfect lamb. He then adds that Jesus was destined for the cross before the foundation of the world. (1 Peter 1:18-20) As Peter introduces the idea of Jesus as the sacrificial lamb, it is an idea sown into the fabric of God's Word from the earlier books of the Old Testament. There are dozens and dozens of verses foretelling the coming of Christ as the Messiah. Here are a few centred on his sacrificial crucifixion:

- "Strike the shepherd, and the sheep will be scattered." (Zechariah 13:7)
- "I gave my back to those who beat me, and my cheeks to those who tore out my beard. I did not hide my face from scorn and spitting." (Isaiah 50:6)
- "They pierced my hands and my feet." (Psalm 22:16)
- "My God, my God, why have you forsaken me?" (Psalm 22:1)
- "Instead they gave me gall for my food, and for my thirst they gave me vinegar to drink." (Psalm 69:21)

- "Yet he himself bore our sicknesses, and he carried our pains; but we in turn regarded him stricken, struck down by God, and afflicted." (Isaiah 53:4)
- "He bore the sin of many and interceded for the rebels." (Isaiah 52:12)
- "He was oppressed and afflicted, yet he did not open his mouth. Like a lamb led to the slaughter and like a sheep silent before her shearers, he did not open his mouth." (Isaiah 53:7)
- "They will look at me whom they pierced." (Zechariah 12:10)

And most telling for this section, this final prophecy, again from Isaiah 53: "He willingly submitted to death." All of those prophecies written hundreds and hundreds of years before the birth of Jesus, and they all speak to the theological truth and historical fact that Jesus Christ was crucified. The true story that the Bible tells stands alone in this regard. There is no other major religious writing in the history of the world with the specific, predictive prophecies such as we find in Christian Scripture. The writings of Buddha, Confucius, Mohammed nor the texts of Hinduism contain any prophecies, yet the Bible contains more than two thousand, most of them already having been fulfilled.[34]

But the prophesying and prediction of the Messiah's crucifixion wasn't just a trait of the Old Testament, the New Testament is replete with evidence that the Messiah was destined for the cross. Providing additional weight to the New Testament's references to the inevitable, sacrificial death comes from the Lord Jesus himself!

As Millard Erickson reveals, the Gospel of John contains several comments spoken by Jesus indicating that his purpose was a salvific one, and that it was a central part of the Kingdom work the Father had sent him to complete.[35] On two different occasions, recorded in John 6:38 and 10:36, Jesus clarifies that He was sent into the world by the Father and that He was there to do the Father's will, "the will of him who sent me."

Perhaps the most famous reference to the salvation work of Christ in John's gospel is found in chapter 3, verses 16 and 17: "For God so loved the world that he gave his only Son, so the everyone who believes in him may not perish, but may have eternal life. Indeed, God did not send the Son into the world to condemn the world, but in order that the world might be saved through him."

A close reading of John's gospel also reveals that others beyond Jesus were made aware of Christ's inevitable death. John the Baptist, seeing Jesus walking towards him declared in prophesy and recognition, "Here is the Lamb of God who takes away the sin of the world!"

During his three-year ministry with the disciples, Jesus often spoke freely and openly about his coming death at the hands of others. "The Son of Man must suffer many things and be rejected by the elders and the chief priests and the scribes and be killed, and after three days rise again" (Mark 8:31; see also Matthew 17:22; Luke 9:22). The Lord also indicated that his enemies would destroy the temple, which he meant as a symbol for his body, but that it would be rebuilt in three days (John 2:19; Mark 14:58; Matthew 26:61).

Jesus shows us clearly that love looks like the cross. As a result of his life and example for us, we also learn that love looks like obedience to God and submission to the will of the Father.

Another common question from critics of the faith is, 'If God really is the God of Love, why would God allow His Son to suffer in such a way?'

The very structure of the question reveals a profound misunderstanding of the nature of God. It implies a separation between Father and Son where no such distance exists. If God the Father and God the Son were two independently individual beings, the posed question would bear discussion and consideration, but that's just not the case.

One of the most profound, and confounding, doctrines of the Christian faith is the reality of the Trinity. This means that the Christian understanding of God is that the deity is a Triune God - three 'persons' (to use the psychological term for agency) but one Being. It is not a dichotomy to say that God is Father, Son and Holy Spirit, but that we have One God. In fact, some of the earliest theology the Bible gives to us confirms this for us. From Deut. 6:4, we have a foundational truth that is the opening of the Shema prayer: "Hear, O Israel: The LORD our God, the LORD is one."

As God is One - Father, Son and Spirit - the certainty of the crucifixion is not, as some controversial critics have insisted, a case of cosmic child abuse. The Father did not inflict, or permit, the pain and humiliation of the cross on a being outside of himself. Truly, as Christ comes to the cross, as God is One, God intimately knew every moment of Jesus' experience.

Let's go back to Jesus' quote from John 13 that opens this chapter. "No one has greater love than this, to lay down one's life for one's friends." What does the cross look like? It looks like love.

God is Love

So far we've talked about the example of love, the Triune reality of God, the plan of salvation enacted through the life and death of Jesus, but there's two more things that we must comment on, truths that the Story of God demands that we address.

The first leads into the second, which takes us back to the cross ... and to the Easter Sunday miracle. But first, everything begins with this truth: God is love, and when we say that, we understand that God's love means that God eternally gives of himself to others.[36] This means that love is self-giving and other-focused, always for the benefit of the other. God then, as part of his nature, gives of himself to be a blessing to others. As discussed above, in Jesus, the second person of the Trinity, we see giving all of himself for the benefit and blessing of others.

While the greatest example of God's love may be his atoning sacrifice and resurrection, we see that the depth, purity and reality of God's love is foundational to all of reality. This attribute of love was present and active even before creation, existing and flourishing among the members of the Trinity. Jesus confirms this for us twice during his great prayer of intercession in John 17. In vs. 5, the Lord refers to the glory that he had while in the Father's presence before the world began. Later in vs. 24 of that same chapter, Jesus again mentions the pre-Creation, active love of God: "Father, I desire that those also, whom you have given me, may be with me where I am, to see my glory, which you have given me because you loved me before the foundation of the world."

Did you notice that in vs. 24, that prayer of Jesus typifies our previously given definition of love? It is not solely for the benefit of the self, but it is directed for the blessing of the other.

While the display of God's love on the cross is truly amazing, it is only the penultimate revelation of his love. Perhaps it's more accurate to say that the Cross is only half the story of God's great love. The most stunning display of God's love for the world was discovered by three women on that first Easter Sunday morning, when they rushed to the tomb expecting to find the beaten, bruised and bloodied body of Jesus, but he was not there!

He had risen from the grave … by the plan and love of God!

It needs to be said at this point, that we make one very important proclamation: This love is available to all, and it is yours even before you make Jesus the Lord of your life. Romans 5:8 contains this beautiful truth: "But God proves his love for us in that while we still were sinners Christ died for us."

The great British preacher, Charles Spurgeon, in a sermon entitled, Love's Commendation, taught this great love of God is not just to be spoken about or theorized, but to be experienced and known in a real, life-changing way. Spurgeon proclaimed: "God's commendation of himself and his love is not in words, but in deeds … Let us learn, then, upon the threshold of our text, that if we would commend ourselves, it must be by deeds, and not by words."[37]

As Jesus tells us that is no greater love, no greater deed, than laying down one's life for one's friends.

Yes God's story, and the story of the Bible is a love story - the greatest love story ever told.

Yes, Love conquers death.

Yes, because God is Love, Love wins.

Love always wins.

Prayer for Our Story

Gracious God, the ever-present, loving Father.

We praise you for being the very source of Love, a love so great that it is made known to us through the nature of Your person. You are perfect community. As the Father, your love holds all things together.

You, Great God, are the One whose amazing love still stirs the hearts of all who look to the stars or the setting sun and wonders who could possibly have created this?

May your Glory and Love be more prevalent in all of our lives.

Lord Jesus, you are the One who was willing to lay down His life for all of Humanity.

So we praise you for accepting humiliation in so many ways. Thank you for accepting the humiliation of being confined to human flesh and blood, leaving your rightful place at the Father's right hand.

When we think of the Cross, our hearts break with shame and gratitude. We know, Lord, that it was our sin, that you bore on the Cross.

And more, we know that it was your Love that held you there.

May you open our eyes, our hearts and our souls to the depth of your love for us, a love so great that not even the tomb could contain it.

Holy Spirit, the One who opens our hearts and our minds to the ever-present love of the Triune God, the Three-in-One and the One-in-Three.

In you, we experience the truth that the love of God means that you are ever and always other focused. As our guide and the epitome of spiritual living, help us to pursue this as our standard for loving others.

May we be open to your move within our lives, and ever open to the deep and abiding truths of God.

Afterword

After the words, The Word
or
Why you should be asking, 'May I tell you a story?'

In the beginning was the Word, and the Word was with God, and the Word was God. He was in the beginning with God.
- John 1:1-2, NRSV

"Go therefore and make disciples of all nations, baptizing them in the name of the Father and of the Son and of the Holy Spirit, and teaching them to obey everything that I have commanded you. And remember, I am with you always, to the end of the age."
- Matthew 28:19-20, NRSV

We began this journey with the intent of reclaiming, and reacquainting ourselves with God's great story, that story that has shaped so much of the reality that we now enjoy and live in.

We have examined family issues, selfishness, greed, friendship, the danger of rash decisions, dealing with enemies, problem avoidance and navigating a rapidly changing culture. Through all of the chapters and topics of this book, there have been two constants: First, we learned that a lot of the time, people, including God's people, aren't very reliable/thoughtful/kind/honest or sensible (feel free to insert your own adjective here). The second constant is the Triune God. Regardless of the situation and the people involved, God is there. Jesus shows up. The Holy Spirit moves.

Because the story goes on, that hasn't changed! God is still there. Jesus still shows up and the Holy Spirit continues to move ... the fact that this book exists and that you are reading it is proof of that.

I know that most of the stories covered in this book will be familiar ones to many of the readers. This was intentional, also purposeful was the (hopefully) unique presentation, giving readers a new avenue into those well-known stories. This was done for two reasons: First, to bolster the readers familiarity with the Biblical texts, and improving an unfortunate situation within the church that this generation of believers must begin to address - the crippling problem of Biblical illiteracy. The second is an even more pressing issue, and it's the response of obedience.

The very last thing that Jesus says to his followers in the Gospel of Matthew is what is known as the Great Commission. In those verses, Jesus commands his people to go to the ends of the earth making disciples in all nations, baptizing them in the name of the Father and of the Son and of the Holy Spirit, teaching them to obey everything that Jesus commanded them. Please read this carefully: This is called the Great Commission not the Great Suggestion, nor the Great Recommendation. By using the word 'commission' there is an implied sense of engagement.

So, lets be engaged! Lets take the Great Commission seriously.

There are 13 chapters in this book, meaning you now have 13 new stories of, and about, God to share with others. In one calendar year, that means you now have one new story that you could share with the ever-increasing number of unchurched people every four weeks. In one year, you could have shared the good news of the Kingdom of God with 13 people. I'm no mathematician, but you can see how if we were all to do this, it would take no time at all to reach a large number of people.

But the best part is that after that one year period, you will need a whole new batch of stories to tell ... and the truly great news of using our Bibles as the source for reaching out to others, is that there are enough fantastic, wonderful, life-changing stories to last more than our lifetimes. And why is that?

Because stories are just collections of words, but Bible stories are always the reflection of the Word.

And that Word is Love - captivating, fascinating, never-ending Love.

Now, get out there and ask someone (or 13 someones) this question: May I tell you a Story?

<u>Prayer for Our Story</u>

God the Father, God the Son, God the Holy Spirit

We praise you as the God of story. Your very Triune nature is the basis for story in and of itself.

How wonderful you are.

We thank you for the gift of story, for the story of your love, your Incarnation, your continuing story, and the fact that we have a role in the story that you are ever-writing on the fabric of reality.

Father, only a heart as pure and vibrant as Yours could conceive of such a story.

Jesus, only a life as pure and holy as Yours could show us how to live into this story.

Holy Spirit, only a love as pure and inclusive as Yours could empower us to invite others into Your great story.

Father, Son, and Spirit, we will love you until The End.

References

Scripture References

Old Testament

Genesis 4:1-10

Exodus 4:27
Exodus 6:28-7:7
Exodus 17:8-15

Numbers 6:24-26
Numbers 22:7-12
Numbers 22:26-30

Deuteronomy 6:4

1 Samuel 13:2
1 Samuel 13:14
1 Samuel 14:24-30
1 Samuel 18:1-5
1 Samuel 18:14
1 Samuel 19:1-3
1 Samuel 20:12-15
1 Samuel 31:2-3
2 Samuel 9:1

Psalm 22:1
Psalm 22:6
Psalm 118:14-17
Psalm 139:8-10

Ecclesiastes 1:9

Isaiah 50:6
Isaiah 52:12
Isaiah 53:4
Isaiah 53:7

Daniel 3:9-12
Daniel 3:17
Daniel 3:29

Jonah 1
Jonah 1:3
Jonah 1:17
Jonah 2

Zechariah 12:10
Zechariah 13:7

Scripture References

New Testament

Matthew 4:19
Matthew 5:14
Matthew 13:3-5
Matthew 14:25-30
Matthew 16:1-4
Matthew 16:16
Matthew 16:23
Matthew 17:22
Matthew 19:24
Matthew 20:16
Matthew 26:35
Matthew 26:61
Matthew 28:19-20

Mark 1:1
Mark 1:6-9
Mark 8:31
Mark 9:5
Mark 9:23
Mark 10:17-27
Mark 11:13-14
Mark 11:20-22
Mark 12:13-17
Mark 14:48-52
Mark 14:58
Mark 15:46
Luke 9:22
Luke 11:29-32
Luke 15:10-14

John 1:46-49
John 2:15
John 2:19
John 3:3
John 3:12
John 3:16-17
John 3:30
John 14:28-29
John 15:10-14
John 15:13
John 17:5
John 17:21
John 17:24
John 18:7-11

Acts 2:3
Acts 2:22-24
Acts 12:12
Acts 13:5
Acts 15:36-39

References

Scripture References

New Testament

Romans 3:23
Romans 13:1

2 Cor. 12:8-10

Colossians 4:10

1 Tim 2:1-4
1 Tim. 6:91 Tim. 6:10

2 Tim 2:17
2 Tim. 4:11

1 Peter 2:11
1 Peter 5:13

1 John 4:16

References

Endnotes

Chapter 1

[1] Laurence A., Turner, Genesis (London, New York: Continuum) 36

Chapter 2

[2] Richard Foster, Life with God (New York: Harper Collins, 2008)

[3] Peter Enns, Exodus: The NIV Application Commentary, (Grand Rapids, Michigan: Zondervan, 2000) 209

[4] https://www.myjewishlearning.com/article/aaron-the-high-priest/

Chapter 3

[5] A.S. Kramer, Three Rabbis in a Rowboat: The World's Best Jewish Humour (New York: Citadel Press, 1996) 29

[6] John F. Walvoord, and Roy B. Zuck, The Bible Knowledge Commentary, (Wheaton, Illinois: Scripture Press Publications, Inc. 1983, 1985).

[7] Ronald B. Allen, Numbers: Genesis, Exodus, Leviticus, Numbers (Grand Rapids, Michigan: Zondervan, 1990)

Chapter 4

[8] Tremper Longman III, and Raymond Dillard, Introduction to the Old Testament (Grand Rapids, Michigan: Zondervan, 2004)

[9] John Goldingay, Old Testament Theology, Volume 1: Israel's Gospel (Downers Grove, Ill., Intervarsity Press, 2003)

[10] J. Denny Weaver, The Nonviolent God (Grand Rapids, Michigan: Eerdmans, 2013)

Chapter 5

[11] C. S. Lewis, The Four Loves (New York, Harcourt Brace and Company, 1960)

[12] Ronald F. Youngblood, 1&2 Samuel: The Expositor's Bible Commentary, (Grand Rapids, Michigan: Zondervan, 1992)

Chapter 6

[13] Gleason L. Archer, Jr., Daniel: The Expositor's Bible Commentary, (Grand Rapids, Michigan: Zondervan, 1992)

[14] Tremper Longman III, and Raymond Dillard, Introduction to the Old Testament (Grand Rapids, Michigan: Zondervan, 2004)

[15] Ibid

[16] W.S. Towner, Daniel (Interp, John Knox, 1984) 21

Chapter 8

[17] Walter W. Wessel, Mark: The Expositor's Bible Commentary, (Grand Rapids, Michigan: Zondervan, 1984)

[18] Ibid

[19] Ibid

[20] David Garland, Mark: The NIV Application Commentary, (Grand Rapids, Michigan: Zondervan, 1996)

[21] R. Kent Hughes, Mark: Jesus, Servant and Saviour: Preaching the Word Commentary, (Wheaton, Illinois: Crossway, 2015)

[22] Ibid

Chapter 9

[23] Ibid

[24] Walter W. Wessel, Mark: The Expositor's Bible Commentary, (Grand Rapids, Michigan: Zondervan, 1984)

[25] Ibid

[26] David Garland, Mark: The NIV Application Commentary, (Grand Rapids, Michigan: Zondervan, 1996)

Chapter 10

[27] William Barclay, The Gospel of Mark, (Philadelphia: Westminster, 1956), 280

[28] R. Kent Hughes, Mark: Jesus, Servant and Saviour: Preaching the Word Commentary, (Wheaton, Illinois: Crossway, 2015), 272

[29] Jesus was citing Isaiah 56:7 and Jeremiah 7:11 in his denunciation of the Temple economy.

[30] R. Kent Hughes, Mark: Jesus, Servant and Saviour: Preaching the Word Commentary, (Wheaton, Illinois: Crossway, 2015), 272

Chapter 11

[31] Adam Hamilton, Simon Peter, (Nashville: Abingdon Press, 2018), 20

[32] D.A. Carson, Matthew: The Expositor's Bible Commentary, (Grand Rapids, Michigan: Zondervan, 1984)

Chapter 12

[33] D.A. Carson, Matthew: The Expositor's Bible Commentary, (Grand Rapids, Michigan: Zondervan, 1984)

Chapter 13

[34] D. James Kennedy, Christ: The Fulfillment of Prophecy, (Nashville, Tennessee: Holman Bible Publishers, 2017)

[35] Millard J. Erickson, Christian Theology, (Grand Rapids, Michigan: Baker Books, 1995)

[36] Wayne Grudem, Systematic Theology (Grand Rapids, Michigan: Zondervan, 1994)

[37] Charles H. Spurgeon, Spurgeon's Sermons, Vol. II (Peabody, Massachusetts: Henderson Publishers Marketing, LLC, 2017)

Manufactured by Amazon.ca
Bolton, ON

23196564R00098